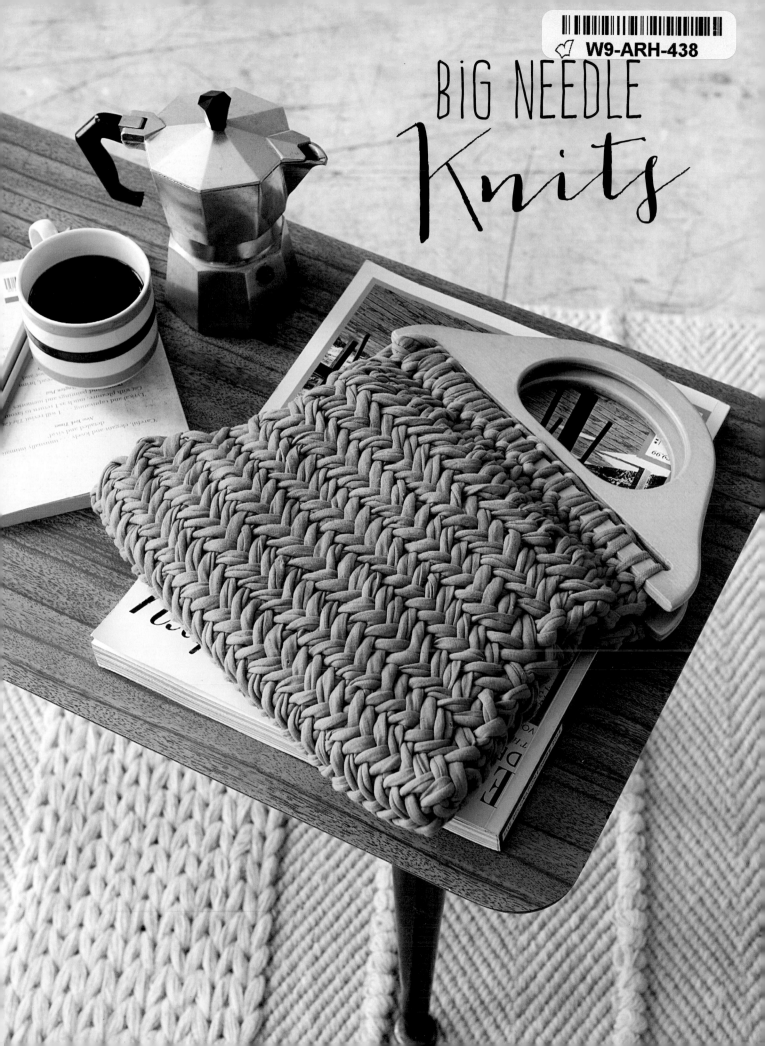

BiG NEEDLE
Knits

BIG NEEDLE
Knits

35 PROJECTS TO KNIT USING SUPER-SIZE NEEDLES

MELANIE PORTER

CICO BOOKS
LONDON NEW YORK

This book is dedicated to Jai and Ellora.
Love, Mummy

Published in 2015 by CICO Books
An imprint of Ryland Peters & Small Ltd
20—21 Jockey's Fields   341 E 116th St
London WC1R 4BW   New York, NY 10029
www.rylandpeters.com

10 9 8 7 6 5 4 3 2 1

A CIP catalog record for this book is available from
the Library of Congress and the British Library.

ISBN: 978 1 78249 253 5

Printed in China

Editor: Katy Denny
Design concept: Geoff Borin
Designer: Sarah Rock
Photographer: Penny Wincer and Emma Mitchell
Stylist: Nel Haynes
Technique illustrators: Stephen Dew, Kuo Kang
Chen, and Kate Simunek

Senior editor: Carmel Edmonds
In-house designer: Fahema Khanam
Art director: Sally Powell
Production controller: Mai-Ling Collyer
Publishing manager: Penny Craig
Publisher: Cindy Richards

Contents

Introduction

Following a ten year career in the fashion industry, I created a homewares brand that focused on using knitted materials to transform vintage furniture and lamps into one-off pieces for the modern home. Inspired by scale and the challenge of knitting in both traditional and unusual materials, such as merino wool, bamboo, and rope, I wrote *Hand-knit Your Home* and *The Hand-knitted Nursery* with easy-to-follow patterns for adventurous knitters.

My favorite projects are often worked on big needles, ranging from US 15 (10mm) to bespoke custom-made 1½in (35mm) diameter needles. These super chunky knits allow you to work easily on a large scale and accentuate the textures of the different stitch structures.

In this book, I have returned to my fashion roots to design 35 projects, which all use big needles to create unique clothing and accessories, with a few of my signature homewares. Information is also included on how you can make your own chunky yarn from cotton or linen fabric, on suppliers of super bulky yarns, and on stitches to knit off-gauge using fine yarn on big needles to create a dense knitted fabric.

I hope you enjoy choosing which patterns to knit and making some fabulous big needle knits of your own.

Melanie Porter

CHAPTER 1

Chunky Textures

Bring tactile texture to your knitting with bobbles, cables, chunky ribbing, and more in these cozy projects. Big needles and thick yarn are the perfect way to showcase textured stitches, so prepare to create giant versions of all your favorite stitch combinations.

Slouch hat

THE FACETED RIBBED PATTERN OF THIS HAT MAKES THE CHUNKY YARN SEEM EVEN THICKER, AND A 2X2 RIB BORDER GIVES A NICE SNUG FIT, SO THERE`S NO CHANCE OF FEELING THE COLD.

SIZE
Approx. 12½in (32cm) high and 19¾in (50cm) circumference, stretching to 25½in (65cm) circumference

MATERIALS
Yarn
Super chunky yarn, designed to be knitted on size US 15 (10mm) or US 17 (12mm) needles, such as Magnum from Cascade—100% Peruvian wool; approx. 123yds (112m) per 8⅞oz (250g) ball.
- Birch Heather (A)—approx. 8¾oz (245g)/120yds (109m)
- Charcoal (B)—approx. ⅛oz (5g)/3yds (3m) OR
- Charcoal (A and B)—approx. 8⅞oz (250g)/123yds (112m)

Needles
Pair of size US 15 (10mm) knitting needles

Other materials
- Tapestry needle

GAUGE (TENSION)
7 sts and 10 rows to 4in (10cm) over st st using US 15 (10mm) needles

ABBREVIATIONS
See page 124.

PATTERN
Main piece
Using A, cast on 36 sts.
Rows 1–6: [K2, p2] to end.
Row 7: [K3, p1] to end.
Row 8: K2, p1, [k3, p1] to last st, k1.
Rep rows 7–8, 16 more times.

Change to B (optional).
Next row: P1, [k2togtbl, p1, k1] to last 3 sts, k2togtbl, p1. 27 sts
Next row: K1, [p1, k2] to last 2 sts, p1, k1.
Next row: [K2, p1] to end.
Next row: [K1, p2tog] to end. 18 sts
Next row: [K1, p1] to end.
Next row: [K1, p1] to end.
Next row: [K2togtbl] to end. 9 sts
Cut yarn, leaving a tail of 24in (60cm), and thread through rem sts, drawing tight to close. Do not fasten off.

TO MAKE UP
Using long end, sew hat together along back seam.

Weave in loose ends and steam lightly to shape.

Big bobble knit snood

THIS CHUNKY KNIT SNOOD IS SUPER SOFT, TO KEEP YOU WARM ALL WINTER, AND THE METALLIC SPECKLES ADD A TOUCH OF ELEGANCE.

SIZE
Approx. 13⅜in (34cm) long x 26¾in (68cm) circumference

MATERIALS
Yarn
Chunky yarn such as Gold Leaf from Lion Brand——90% Acrylic, 10% Wool; approx. 49yds (45m) per 2¾oz (75g) ball.
- Grey/Silver——6⅝oz (190g)/126yds (115m)

Needles
US 17 (12mm) 31½in (80cm) long circular knitting needle

Other materials
- Tapestry needle

GAUGE (TENSION)
8 sts and 9 rows to 4in (10cm) over st st using US 17 (12mm) needles.

ABBREVIATIONS
See page 124.

PATTERN
Main piece
Worked with WS facing.
Cast on 56 sts.
Rounds 1–2: [K2, p2] to end. (2x2 rib)
Round 3: Knit.
Round 4: *[K1, p1, k1] all into next st, p3tog*, rep from * to * to end.
Rounds 5–7: Knit.
Round 8: *P3tog, [k1, p1, k1] all into next st*, rep from * to * to end.
Rounds 9–11: Knit.
Rep rounds 4–11, 3 more times.
Rep rounds 4–5.
Next round: [K2, p2] to end.
Next round: [K2, p2] to end.
Bind (cast) off in rib (see page 112).

TO MAKE UP
Weave in all loose ends. Steam lightly to shape.

Turn RS out.

TIP
When knitting on circular needles it is important to check that the cast-on stitches are not twisted before embarking on row 1.

Boot toppers

THESE COZY CUFFS FIT AT THE TOP OF A PAIR OF CALF- OR KNEE-LENGTH BOOTS TO KEEP THE COLD OUT ON CHILLY DAYS. QUICK TO KNIT AND EASY TO WEAR, YOU COULD CREATE SEVERAL PAIRS IN YOUR FAVORITE COLORS.

SIZE
Small (S) Approx. 5in (13cm) high and 12½in (32cm) circumference, stretching to 16¼in (41cm) circumference
Medium (M) Approx. 5in (13cm) high and 14¼in (36cm) circumference, stretching to 19in (48cm) circumference

MATERIALS
Yarn
Super chunky yarn, designed to be knitted on size US 15 (10mm) or US 17 (12mm) needles, such as Magnum from Cascade—100% Peruvian wool; approx. 123yds (112m) per 8⅞ oz (250g) ball.
• Denim—S approx. 2¾oz (80g)/38yds (35m), M approx. 3½oz (100g)/50yds (45m)

Needles
Pair of size US 15 (10mm) knitting needles
Pair of size US 13 (9mm) knitting needles

Other materials
• Tapestry needle

GAUGE (TENSION)
7 sts and 10 rows to 4in (10cm) over st st using US 15 (10mm) needles

ABBREVIATIONS
See page 124.

PATTERN
Main piece S(M)
Using size US 13 (9mm) needles cast on 20(24) sts.
Row 1: Knit.
Row 2: Purl.
Rep rows 1–2, twice more.
Change to size US 15 (10mm) needles.
Row 7: [K3, p1] to end.
Row 8: K2, p1, [k3, p1] to last st, k1.
Rep rows 7–8, 3 more times.
Bind (cast) off.

TO MAKE UP
Join side seams together. Weave in loose ends and steam lightly to shape.

TIP

I suggest using size US 13 (9mm) needles for the first 6 rows to keep the knit nice and snug inside the boot and to reduce any pilling caused by the boot. If you do not have both sizes of needles you could use the size US 15 (10mm) pair from the start, and knit the first 6 rows at a tighter tension.

Clutch bag

PERFECTLY SIZED TO HOLD EXACTLY WHAT YOU NEED FOR AN EVENING OUT, THIS
CUTE PURSE IS AS ELEGANT AS IT IS PRACTICAL.

SIZE
Approx. 10½in (27cm) wide x 7½in
(19cm) high

MATERIALS
Yarn
Chunky yarn such as Cocoon from Rowan—
80% Merino, 20% kid mohair; approx.
126yds (115m) per 3½oz (100g) ball.
- Kiwi OR Seascape (A)—approx. 4½oz
  (125g)/162yds (144m)
- Clay (B)—approx. 1oz (30g)/36yds (35m)

Needles
Pair of size US 15 (10mm) knitting needles

Other materials
- Tapestry needle
- Lining fabric measuring 19¾in (50cm) x
  10¾in (27.5cm)
- Sewing needle
- Sewing thread to match fabric
- Stiff facing fabric 19¼in (49cm) x 10in
  (26cm)
- Button or tie for closure

GAUGE (TENSION)
9 sts and 12 rows to 4in (10cm) over st st
using US 15 (10mm) needles

ABBREVIATIONS
Sl1 wyb—slip 1 st purlwise with yarn at back
Sl1 wyf—slip 1 st purlwise with yarn at front
See also page 124.

PATTERN
Main piece
Work with 2 ends of yarn throughout the
pattern.
Using A, cast on 30 sts.
Row 1: [K1, sl1 wyf] to end.
Row 2: [P1, sl1 wyb] to end.
Rep rows 1—2 until your work measures
approx. 13½in (34cm).

Change to B.
Next row: [K1, sl1 wyf] to end.
Next row: [P1, sl1 wyb] to end.

Change to A.
Next row: [K1, sl1 wyf] to end.
Next row: [P1, sl1 wyb] to end.
Repeat the last 4 rows, 4 more times.

Change to B.
Next row: [K1, sl1 wyf] 7 times, bind (cast) off
2 sts, sl1 wyf, [k1, sl1 wyf] to end. 28 sts
Next row: [P1, sl1 wyb] 7 times, [k1, p1, k1]
into the next st, sl1 wyb, [p1, sl1 wyb] to end.
30 sts

Change to A.
Next row: [K1, sl1 wyf] to end.
Next row: [P1, sl1 wyb] to end.

Change to B.
Next row: [K1, sl1 wyf] to end.
Next row: [P1, sl1 wyb] to end.
Bind (cast) off: K1, sl1, pass first st over second st, [k1, pass first st over second st, sl1, pass first st over second st] to end.

TO MAKE UP
Hand stitch the facing fabric to the back of knitted panel to stop any stretching. Sew ¼in (5mm) from the edge.

Fold the bottom third of the flat piece upward, with the facing on the inside, leaving the two-color part as a single layer at the top so that it can fold down as a flap. Stitch the side seams closed.

Fold the lining fabric to fit the bag with right sides together, and stitch the side seams. Press the seams open, and press raw edges under by ¼in (5mm). Use slip stitch to secure the lining to the bag around the opening and flap, covering the facing.

Cut a small opening in the lining fabric and the facing fabric at the buttonhole position and stitch around the edge of the hole.

Attach a button or fabric tie on the front of the bag so that it passes through the buttonhole.

Big bobble knit muff

ADD A GLAMOROUS VINTAGE TOUCH TO YOUR WINTER LOOK WITH THIS BOBBLE KNIT MUFF. SPECKS OF METALLIC FOIL THROUGH THE YARN MAKE THIS PERFECT ATTIRE FOR A COLD EVENING OUT.

SIZE
Approx. 17¾ in (45cm) long x 21¾in (55cm) circumference at widest point

MATERIALS
Yarn
Chunky yarn such as Gold Leaf from Lion Brand—90% Acrylic, 10% Wool; approx. 49yds (45m) per 2¾oz (75g) ball.
• White/Gold—4¾oz (135g)/ 88½yds (81m)

Needles
Size US 17 (12mm) 23½ or 31½in (60cm or 80cm) long circular knitting needle
Size US 15 (10mm) 23½ or 31½in (60cm or 80cm) long circular knitting needle

Other materials
• Tapestry needle
• 14in (36cm) x 24in (61cm) lining fabric (I used a white piece of knitted fabric from a woolen sweater.)
• Matching sewing thread
• Sewing needle

GAUGE (TENSION)
8 sts and 9 rows to 4in (10cm) over st st using US 17 (12mm) needles.

ABBREVIATIONS
See page 124.

PATTERN
Main piece
Worked with WS facing.
Using US 15 (10mm) circular needle cast on 24 sts.
Rounds 1—8: [K2, p2] to end. (2x2 rib)
Transfer sts onto US 17 (12mm) circular needle.
Round 9: [K2, inc 1] to end. 32 sts
Round 10: *[K1, p1, k1] all into next st, p3tog*, rep from * to * to end.
Rounds 11—13: Knit.
Round 14: * P3tog, [K1, p1, k1] all into next st*, rep from * to * to end.
Rounds 15—17: Knit.
Round 18: *[K1, p1, k1] all into next st, p3tog*, rep from * to * to end.
Round 19: [K3, inc 1] to end. 40 sts
Rounds 20—21: Knit.
Round 22: *P3tog, [k1, p1, k1] all into next st*, rep from * to * to end.
Rounds 23—25: Knit.
Round 26: *[K1, p1, k1] all into next st, p3tog*, rep from * to * to end.
Rounds 27 29: Knit.
Round 30: *P3tog, [k1, p1, k1] all into next st*, rep from * to * to end.

Round 31: [K2tog, k3] to end. 32 sts
Rounds 32–33: Knit.
Round 34: *[k1, p1, k1] all into next st, p3tog*, rep from * to * to end.
Rounds 35–37: Knit.
Round 38: *P3tog, [k1, p1, k1] all into next st*, rep from * to * to end.
Round 39: [K2, k2tog] to end. 24 sts
Rounds 40–46: [K2, p2] to end. (2x2 rib)
Bind (cast) off in rib (see page 112).

TO MAKE UP

Weave in all ends and steam lightly to shape.

Turn RS out.

Fold finished muff flat with wrong sides together and sides aligned. Place on a large sheet of paper and trace around it to create a paper pattern to fit the body of the muff (excluding the cuff).

Fold lining fabric in half, place paper pattern on top and cut the fabric around the paper pattern with ⅜in (1cm) seam allowance. Place fabric pieces right sides together and stitch both long seams.

With wrong sides together, slip the lining inside the muff and pin where the cuff joins the bramble stitch. Turning a small hem of the lining under, hand stitch the lining to the knitted muff.

TIP

I used a matching lining to keep the muff a single color, but as the bobble stitch is an open knit, using a contrast color lining would give a striking modern finish.

Braided scarf

AN UNUSUAL BRAID PATTERN MAKES THIS SCARF A REAL ONE-OFF. THE LOVELY THICK YARN WILL KEEP YOU TOASTY IN THE COLDEST WEATHER.

SIZE
Approx. 6in (15cm) x 70in (178cm)

MATERIALS
Yarn
Super chunky yarn designed to be knitted on size US 15 (10mm) or US 17 (12mm) needles, such as Magnum from Cascade— 100% Peruvian Wool; approx. 123yds/112m per 8⅞oz (250g) ball.
• Gold—13⅛oz (375g)/184yds (168m)

Needles
Pair of size US 17 (12mm) knitting needles

Other materials
• Tapestry needle

GAUGE (TENSION)
7 sts and 8 rows to 4in (10cm) over st st using US 17 (12mm) needles

ABBREVIATIONS
See page 124.

PATTERN
Main piece
Cast on 18 sts.
Row 1 (RS): Knit.
Row 2: Purl.
Rep rows 1–2, 3 more times.
Row 9: C12F, k6.
Row 10: Purl.
Rep rows 1–2, twice more.
Row 15: K6, C12B.
Row 16: Purl.
Rep rows 5–16, 11 more times or until the work measures approx. 67in (170cm).
Next row: Knit.
Next row: Purl.
Rep last 2 rows, twice more.
Bind (cast) off.

TO MAKE UP
Weave in all loose ends. Steam lightly to shape.

TIP
If you want to make this scarf even longer repeat rows 5–16 until you reach the required length.

Herringbone legwarmers

THESE LEGWARMERS IN A BEAUTIFUL HERRINGBONE STITCH PATTERN WILL KEEP YOU WONDERFULLY WARM IN EFFORTLESS STYLE. GREAT WORN WITH LEATHER BOOTS ON COLD DAYS.

SIZE
Approx. 9¾in (25cm) circumference x 13in (33cm) high

MATERIALS
Yarn
Chunky yarn such as Cocoon from Rowan—80% Merino, 20% kid mohair; approx. 126yds (115m) per 3½oz (100g) ball.
- Tundra—approx. 4½oz (125g)/158yds (144m)

Needles
Pair of size US 15 (10mm) knitting needles
Pair of size US 10½ (7mm) knitting needles

Other materials
- Tapestry needle

GAUGE (TENSION)
16 sts and 11 rows to 4in (10cm) over Herringbone st using US 15 (10mm) needles

ABBREVIATIONS
See page 124.

PATTERN
Main piece
Make two
Using US 10½ (7mm) needles cast on 40 sts.
Rows 1–8: [K2, p2] to end. (2x2 rib)
Change to US 15 (10mm) needles.
Row 9 (RS): [K2togtbl dropping only the first st off left needle] to end, k rem st on left needle.
Row 10: [P2tog dropping only the first st off left needle] to end, p rem st on left needle.
Rep rows 9–10, 11 more times.
Next row: Rep row 9.
Change to US 10½ (7mm) needles.
Next row: Rep row 10.
Rep rows 1–8.
Bind (cast) off in rib (see page 112).

TO MAKE UP
Sew back seams. Weave in loose ends and steam lightly to shape.

TIP
Keep the cast-on and bound-(cast-) off rows loose to allow for stretch, or use a size larger needles for those 2 rows.

TIP

To stop the different color yarn balls getting tangled, place each one in a different container on the floor because you will have three colors attached to the work at the same time.

Multi-strand blanket

YOU'LL LOVE TO SNUGGLE UNDER THIS SUPER COZY THROW ON A COLD EVENING.
THE BOLD CHECK PATTERN MAKES IT A CONTEMPORARY HOMEWARE DESIGN.

SIZE
Approx. 50in (127cm) x 34¼in (87cm)

MATERIALS
Yarn
Super chunky yarn designed to be knitted on size US 15 (10mm) or US 17 (12mm) needles, such as Magnum from Cascade—100% Peruvian Wool; approx. 123yds (112m) per 8⅞oz (250g) ball.
- Lake Chelan Heather (A)—15⅞oz (450g)/ 221yds (202m)
- Koala Bear (B)—8⅞oz (250g)/ 123yds (112m)
- Ecru (C)—8⅞oz (250g)/123yds (112m)

Needles
Pair of size US 35 (20mm) knitting needles

Other materials
- Tapestry needle

GAUGE (TENSION)
5 sts and 7 rows to 4in (10cm) over st st using US 35 (20mm) needles.

ABBREVIATIONS
Sl1 wyf—slip 1 st purlwise with yarn at front
Sl1 wyb—slip 1 st purlwise with yarn at back
See also page 124.

PATTERN
Border
Using A, cast on 58 sts.
Row 1 (RS): [K1, sl1 wyf] to end.
Row 2: [P1, sl1 wyb] to end.
Rep rows 1–2, 5 more times.

Main piece
Change to B.
Row 13: [K1, sl1 wyf] to end.
Change to C.
Row 14: [P1, sl1 wyb] to end.
Change to A.
Row 15: [K1, sl1 wyf] to end.
Change to B.
Row 16: [P1, sl1 wyb] to end.
Change to C.
Row 17: [K1, sl1 wyf] to end.
Change to A.
Row 18: [P1, sl1 wyb] to end.

Rep rows 13–18 until your blanket measures approx. 45¾in (116cm) (or until colors B or C run out.)

Border
Change to A.
Rep rows 1–2, 5 times.
Rep row 1.
Bind (cast) off.

TO MAKE UP
Weave in all loose ends. Steam lightly to shape.

Cable headband

PERFECT FOR KEEPING YOUR EARS SHIELDED FROM THE WINTER WIND, THIS LOVELY CABLE HEADBAND DOUBLES UP AS A STYLISH HAIR ACCESSORY TO TAME YOUR LOCKS.

SIZE
Approx. 5½in (14cm) wide and 19¾in (50cm) circumference, stretching to 23¾in (60cm) circumference

MATERIALS
Yarn
Super chunky yarn, designed to be knitted on size US 15 (10mm) or US 17 (12mm) needles, such as Magnum from Cascade—100% Peruvian wool; approx. 123yds (112m) per 8⅞oz (250g) ball.
• Strawberries and Cream—2¾oz (80g)/38yds (35m)

Needles
Pair of size US 17 (12mm) knitting needles

Other materials
• Cable needle
• 2 stitch holders
• Tapestry needle

GAUGE (TENSION)
7 sts and 8 rows to 4in (10cm) over st st using US 17 (12mm) needles

ABBREVIATIONS
See page 124.

PATTERN
Main piece
Cast on 14 sts.
Row 1: K2, p2, k6, p2, k2.
Row 2: P2, k2, p6, k2, p2.
Rep rows 1—2, twice more.
Row 7: K2, p2, C6F, p2, k2.
Rep rows 2—7.
Rep rows 2—6. 18 rows
Next row: K2, p2, k2. Place these 6 sts onto first stitch holder and continue working on the rem sts. Bind (cast) off 2 sts knitwise, k1, p2, k2. 6 sts
Work 6 rows as each st presents. Break yarn. Transfer these 6 sts onto second stitch holder and on WS replace original 6 sts onto working needle.
Work 6 rows as each st presents. Place sts back onto first stitch holder.
On WS cross right hand sts in front of left hand sts and replace onto working needle in new order.
Next row (WS): P2, k2, p2, [k1, p1, k1] all into next st, p1, k2, p2.
Rep rows 1—18
Bind (cast) off.

TO MAKE UP
Using mattress st join cast-on and bound-(cast-) off ends to form headband.

Weave in all loose ends. Steam lightly to shape.

Cable fingerless gloves

CHUNKY YARN AND A FUN CABLE MAKE THESE GLOVES GREAT FASHION ACCESSORIES, AND THE FINGERLESS STYLE MAKES THEM HUGELY PRACTICAL.

SIZE
Approx. 9¾in (25cm) x 9½in (24cm) circumference

MATERIALS
Yarn
Super chunky yarn designed to be knitted on size US 15 (10mm) or US 17 (12mm) needles, such as Magnum from Cascade—100% Peruvian Wool; approx. 123yds/112m per 8⅞oz (250g) ball.
• Blue Hawaii—4⅜oz (125g)/61yds (56m)

Needles
Pair of size US 15 (10mm) knitting needles

Other materials
• Cable needle
• Tapestry needle

GAUGE (TENSION)
7 sts and 10 rows to 4in (10cm) over st st using US 15 (10mm) needles.

ABBREVIATIONS
BO—bind (cast) off
Turn—turn the knitting as though you have completed the row
CO—cast on
See also page 124.

PATTERN
Right glove
Cast on 20 sts using thumb method (see page 109).
Rows 1–6: [P2, k2] to end. (2x2 rib)
Row 7: P2, k2, p1, k8, p1, k2, p2, k2.
Row 8: P2, k2, p2, k1, p8, k1, p2, k2.
Rows 9–10: Rep rows 7–8.
Row 11: P2, k2, p1, C4F, C4B, p1, k2, p2, k2.
Row 12: P2, k2, p2, k1, p8, k1, p2, k2.
Rep rows 9–12.
Rep rows 9–11.
Row 20: P2, k1, BO 3 sts knitwise, p8, k1, p2, k2. 17 sts
Row 21: P2, k1, p1, k8, p1, turn, CO 2 sts, turn, p1, k2. 19 sts
Row 22: P2, k2, p1, k1, p8, k1, p2, k2.
Row 23: P2, k2, p1, C4F, C4B, p1, k1, p2, k2.
Row 24: P2, k2, p1, k1, p8, k1, p2, k2.
Row 25: P2, k2, p1, k8, p1, k1, p2, k2.
Bind (cast) off.

TIP
Use mattress st to join the side seams to create an invisible seam that will stretch with the body of the knitting.

Left glove

Cast on 20 sts using thumb method (see page 109).
Rows 1–6: [K2, p2] to end. (2x2 rib)
Row 7: K2, p2, k2, p1, k8, p1, k2, p2.
Row 8: K2, p2, k1, p8, k1, p2, k2, p2.
Rows 9–10: Rep rows 7–8.
Row 11: K2, p2, k2, p1, C4F, C4B, p1, k2, p2.
Row 12: K2, p2, k1, p8, k1, p2, k2, p2.
Rep rows 9–12.
Rep rows 9–11.
Row 20: K2, p2, k1, p8, k1, BO 3 sts knitwise, p2. 17 sts

Row 21: K2, p1, turn, CO 2 sts, turn, p1, k8, p1, k2, p2. 19 sts
Row 22: K2, p2, k1, p8, k1, p1, k2, p2.
Row 23: K2, p2, k1, p1, C4F, C4B, p1, k2, p2.
Row 24: K2, p2, k1, p8, k1, p1, k2, p2.
Row 25: K2, p2, k1, p1, k8, p1, k2, p2.
Bind (cast) off.

TO MAKE UP

Join side seams. Weave in loose ends and steam lightly to shape.

Linen stitch hat

THIS TWO-COLOR BEANIE IS THE PERFECT HAT TO POP OUT IN ON A COLD DAY.
KNITTED WITH TWO ENDS OF YARN IT IS NICE AND COZY, WHILE NOT TOO BULKY.

SIZE
Approx. 9in (23cm) high and 19¾in (50cm)
circumference, stretching to 25in (64cm)
circumference

MATERIALS
Yarn
Chunky yarn such as Cocoon from Rowan—
80% Merino, 20% kid mohair; approx.
126yds (115m) per 3½oz (100g) ball.
• Bilberry (A)—2¾oz (78g)/99yds (90m)
• Clay (B)   1½oz (42g)/54yds (48m)

Needles
Pair of size US 15 (10mm) knitting needles

Other materials
• Tapestry needle

GAUGE (TENSION)
9 sts and 12 rows to 4in (10cm) over st st
using US 15 (10mm) needles

ABBREVIATIONS
Sl1 wyf—slip 1 st purlwise with yarn at front
Sl1 wyb—slip 1 st purlwise with yarn at back
See also page 124.

PATTERN

Main piece

Using A, cast on 48 sts loosely using thumb method (see page 109).

Rows 1–4: [K2, p2] to end. (2x2 rib)

Change to B.

Row 5 (RS): [K1, sl1 wyf] to end.

Row 6: [P1, sl1 wyb] to end.

Change to A.

Row 7: [K1, sl1 wyf] to end.

Row 8: [P1, sl1 wyb] to end.

Change to B.

Rows 9–32: Rep rows 5–8, 6 more times.

Row 33: [K1, sl1 wyf] to end.

Row 34: [P3tog, sl1 wyb, p1, sl1 wyb, p1, sl1 wyb] to end. 36 sts

Change to A.

Row 35: [K1, sl1 wyf] to end.

Row 36: [P1, sl1 wyb] to end.

Change to B.

Row 37: [K1, sl1 wyf] to end.

Row 38: [P3tog, sl1 wyb, p1, sl1 wyb] to end. 24 sts

Change to A.

Row 39: [K1, sl1 wyf] to end.

Row 40: [P1, sl1 wyb] to end.

Change to B.

Row 41: [K1, sl1 wyf] to end.

Row 42: [P3tog, sl1 wyb] to end. 12 sts

Change to A.

Row 43: [K1, sl1 wyf] to end.

Row 44: [P1, sl1 wyb] to end.

Change to B.

Row 45: [K1, sl1 wyf] to end.

Row 46: [P3tog] to end. 4 sts

Cut yarn, leaving a tail of 24in (60cm), and thread through rem sts, drawing tight to close. Do not fasten off.

TO MAKE UP

Using long end, join back seam.

Weave in all loose ends. Steam lightly to shape.

TIP

When working with two ends of yarn, pull one end from the center of the ball, and the other end from the outside, and knit both at the same time.

Bramble stitch purse

STRUGGLING TO FIND THE PERFECT PURSE TO MATCH YOUR OUTFIT? KNIT ONE IN EVERY COLOR WITH THIS CUTE AND PRACTICAL PATTERN.

SIZE

6in (15cm) x 4in (10cm)

MATERIALS

Yarn

Chunky yarn such as Gold Leaf from Lion Brand—90% acrylic, 10% wool; approx. 49yds (45m) per 2¾oz (75g) ball.

- Teal/Gold—1oz (30g)/20yds (18m)

Needles

Pair of size US 15 (10mm) knitting needles

Other materials

- Tapestry needle
- Sewing needle
- Sewing thread to match color of yarn
- 4in (10cm) long zipper
- 5¾in (14.5cm) x 8in (20cm) lining fabric (I used a matching color cotton)

GAUGE (TENSION)

9 sts and 10 rows to 4in (10cm) over st st using US 15 (10mm) needles

ABBREVIATIONS

See page 124.

PATTERN

Main piece

Cast on 14 sts.

Row 1: Purl.

Row 2: K1, *[k1, p1, k1] all into next st, p3tog*, rep from * to * to last st, k1.

Row 3: Purl.

Row 4: K1, *p3tog, [k1, p1, k1] all into next st*, rep from * to * to last st, k1.

Rep rows 1–4, 4 more times.

Rep rows 1–3.

Bind (cast) off.

TIP

I used a matching color lining to keep my purse a single color. As the bobble knit stitch is an open structure, using a contrast color lining would give a different finish.

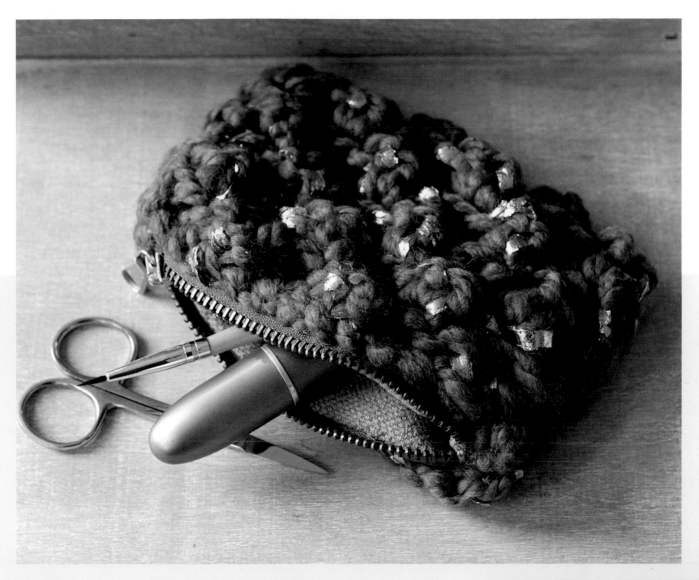

TO MAKE UP

Weave in all loose ends.

Fold knitted piece in half and stitch side seams closed using mattress stitch (see page 119).

Using a sewing needle and sewing thread, stitch the zipper to the opening in the knitted piece.

Fold the lining fabric in half so that its shape is the same as the knitted purse, and stitch the side seams closed so that the lining pocket will be slightly smaller than the knitted piece.

With wrong sides together slip the lining pocket inside the knitted purse and pin at the opening, turning the raw edge of the lining under. Stitch the lining to the zipper tape.

Herringbone vest top

ADD COLOR AND TEXTURE WITH THIS FABULOUS HERRINGBONE KNIT VEST TOP—SO EASY TO WEAR OVER A SHIRT OR LONG-SLEEVED T-SHIRT.

SIZE
To fit bust 34—40in (86—102cm)
Length approx. 22in (56cm)

MATERIALS
Yarn
Chunky yarn such as Cocoon from Rowan—80% Merino, 20% kid mohair; approx. 126yds (115m) per 3½oz (100g) ball.
• Kiwi—14oz (400g)/504yds (460m)

Needles
Pair of size US 15 (10mm) knitting needles
Pair of size US 10½ (7mm) knitting needles

Other materials
• Tapestry needle

GAUGE (TENSION)
16 sts and 11 rows to 4in (10cm) over Herringbone st using US 15 (10mm) needles

ABBREVIATIONS
See page 124.

PATTERN
Back
Using US 10½ (7mm) needles cast on 76 sts.
Rows 1—6: [K2, p2] to end. (2x2 rib)
Change to US 15 (10mm) needles.
Row 7 (RS): [K2togtbl dropping only the first st off left needle] to end, k rem st on left needle.
Row 8: [P2tog, dropping only the first st off left needle] to end, p rem st on left needle.
Rep rows 7—8 until the work measures 15in (38cm), ending with an 8th row.

Shape armholes:
Next row: Bind (cast) off 5 sts, [k2togtbl, dropping only the first st off your needle] to end, k rem st on left needle. 71 sts
Next row: Bind (cast) off 5 sts, [p2tog, dropping only the first st off left needle] to end, p rem st on left needle. 66 sts
Next row: K2togtbl, [k2togtbl, dropping only the first st off left needle] to last 2 sts, k2tog. 64 sts
Next row: P2tog, [p2tog, dropping only the first st off left needle) to last 2 sts, p2tog. 62 sts
Rep last 2 rows. 58 sts
Rep rows 7—8, 7 more times.
Bind (cast) off.

Front

Using US 10½ (7mm) needles cast on 76 sts.
Rows 1–6: [K2, p2] to end. (2x2 rib)
Change to US 15 (10mm) needles.
Row 7: [K2togtbl dropping only the first st off left needle] to end, k rem st on left needle.
Row 8: [P2tog dropping only the first st off left needle] to end, p rem st on left needle.
Rep rows 7–8 until the work measures 15in (38cm), ending with row 8.

Shape armholes:
Next row: Bind (cast) off 5 sts, [k2togtbl dropping only the first st off left needle] to end, k rem st on left needle. 71 sts
Next row: Bind (cast) off 5 sts, [p2tog dropping only the first st off left needle] to end, p rem st on left needle. 66 sts
Next row: K2togtbl, [k2togtbl dropping only the first st off left needle] to last 2 sts, k2tog. 64 sts
Next row: P2tog, [p2tog dropping only the first st off left needle] to last 2 sts, p2tog. 62 sts
Rep last 2 rows. 58 sts
Rep rows 7–8, 3 more times.

Shape neck:
Next row: [K2togtbl dropping only the first st off left needle] 22 times, put the 22 worked sts onto a st holder, bind (cast) off 14 sts, [k2togtbl dropping only the first st off left needle] to end, k rem st on left needle. 22 sts

Next row: [P2tog dropping only the first st off left needle] to last 4 sts, p2tog, p2tog. 20 sts
Next row: K2togtbl, k2togtbl, [k2tog dropping only the first st off left needle] to end. 18 sts
Next row: [P2tog dropping only the first st off left needle] to last 4 sts, p2tog, p2tog. 16 sts
Next row: K2togtbl, k2togtbl, [k2tog dropping only the first st off left needle] to end, k rem st on left needle. 14 sts
Next row: [P2tog dropping only the first st off left needle] to last 4 sts, p2tog, p2tog. 12 sts
Rep rows 7–8 once more.
Bind (cast) off.

Put 22 sts back on needle in direction to start knitting from neckline, rejoin yarn.
Next row: P2tog, p2tog, [p2tog dropping only the first st off left needle] to end, p rem st on left needle. 20 sts
Next row: [K2togtbl dropping only the first st off left needle] to last 4 sts, k2tog, k2tog. 18 sts
Next row: P2tog, p2tog [p2tog, dropping only the first st off left needle] to end, p rem st on left needle. 16 sts
Next row: [K2tog dropping only the first st off left needle] to last 4 sts, k2tog, k2tog. 14 sts
Next row: P2tog, p2tog [p2tog dropping only the first st off left needle] to end, p rem st on left needle. 12 sts
Rep rows 7–8 once more.
Bind (cast) off.

TO MAKE UP

Join front to back at right shoulder seam.

Work neckband: using US 10½ (7mm) needles pick up and k 76 sts evenly distributed around neckline, leaving left shoulder open (12 sts).
Row 1: [K1, p1] to end.
Row 2: [K1, p1] to end.
Bind (cast) off loosely in rib

Join left shoulder seam.

Work armbands: using US 10½ (7mm) needles pick up and k 52 sts evenly distributed around armhole.
Row 1: [K1, p1] to end.
Row 2: [K1, p1] to end.
Bind (cast) off loosely in rib.
Rep on other armhole.

Join side seams.

Weave in all loose ends. Steam lightly to shape.

TIP
Keep the cast on and bound (cast) off rows loose to allow for stretch, or use a size larger needles for those two rows.

CHAPTER 2

Lighter Knits

Love chunky knits even in warm weather? This chapter has all the inspiration you need for whipping up airy, summery creations on big needles. You'll even find projects that use handmade yarn made from cut linen cloth for the ultimate in keeping cool in the sunshine.

Fabric knitted bracelets

EASY TO KNIT IN ANY FABRIC, THESE CHUNKY BRACELETS ARE FAST AND FUN
TO MAKE, AND GREAT AS GIFTS.

SIZE
Thin bracelet—approx. ¾in (2cm) wide x
8¼in (21cm) inner circumference
Thick bracelet—approx. 1¼in (3cm) wide x
8¼in (21cm) inner circumference

MATERIALS
Yarn
½in (1.5cm) wide handmade yarn, made
from cut fabric. See page 123 for cutting
instructions.
- Thin bracelet—approx. ½oz (15g)/6yds
  (5.5m), depending on type of fabric
- Thick bracelet—approx. ¾oz (20g)/9¼yds
  (8.5m) depending on type of fabric

Needles
Pair of size US 15 (10mm) knitting needles

Other materials
- Tapestry needle
- Sewing needle
- Strong sewing thread

GAUGE (TENSION)
10 sts and 12 rows to 4in (10cm) over st st
using US 15 (10mm) needles

ABBREVIATIONS
See page 124.

PATTERN
Thin bracelet
Cast on 20 sts.
Row 1: Knit.
Row 2: Purl.
Bind (cast) off purlwise.

Thick bracelet
Cast on 20 sts.
Row 1: Knit.
Row 2: Purl.
Rep rows 1—2.
Bind (cast) off purlwise.

TO MAKE UP
Weave in loose ends and using strong sewing
thread stitch side seams together to form hoop.

Stitch cast-on edge to bound- (cast-) off edge
with strong sewing thread to create tubular
bracelet shape.

TIP

Make a selection in
different fabrics and wear them
together for a funky look.

TIP

Jersey yarn is made from offcuts from different fabrics, meaning that the elasticity of the yarn varies. Rather than following the gauge (tension) instructions too strictly, find a gauge which feels comfortable for you to knit.

Summer cowl

PERFECT FOR A COOL SUMMER DAY, THIS TEXTURED COWL IS FABULOUSLY COZY WITHOUT LOOKING WINTRY.

SIZE
Approx. 6in (15cm) wide and 47in (120cm) circumference

MATERIALS
Yarn
T-shirt yarn such as Boodles from Hobby Craft—100% Cotton jersey; approx. 99yds (9m) per 1lb (450g) cone. Length depends on the fabric the yarn is made from.
• Neon Pink—approx. 14oz (900g)/ 87yds (80m)

Needles
Size US 19 (15mm) 31½in (80cm) long circular knitting needle

GAUGE (TENSION)
8 sts and 9 rows to 4in (10cm) over st st using US 19 (15mm) needles

ABBREVIATIONS
See page 124.

PATTERN
Main piece
Worked with WS facing.
Cast on 72 sts.
Round 1: Knit.
Round 2: [(K1, p1, k1) all into next st, p3tog] to end.
Round 3: Knit.
Round 4: [P3tog, (k1, p1, k1) all into next st] to end.
Rep rounds 1–4, twice more.
Rep rounds 1–2.
Bind (cast) off.

TO MAKE UP
Weave in all loose ends. Turn RS out.

TIP

Match the lining fabric to
one of the yarn colors to create
a flawless piece.

Jersey pouffe

IDEAL AS A SUPER STYLISH FOOTSTOOL, OR TO BRING OUT WHEN YOU HAVE MORE GUESTS THAN COUCH SPACE. NO LIVING ROOM IS COMPLETE WITHOUT A CHUNKY KNITTED POUFFE!

SIZE
Approx. 19in (48cm) diameter x 8in (20cm) high

MATERIALS
Yarn
Stretchy jersey fabric yarn such as Hoopla Yarn from Hoopla—100% cotton jersey; approx. 109yds (100m) per 1lb 1½oz (500g) cone. Weight depends on the fabric the yarn is made from.
- Mustard (A)— approx. 2lbs 3oz (1kg)/ 219yds (200m)
- Mocha (B)—approx. 1lb 1½oz (500g)/ 109yds (100m)

Needles
Pair of size US 35 (20mm) knitting needles

Other materials
- Lining fabric cut into 2 circles measuring 21½in (55cm) in diameter
- Sewing machine
- Sewing needle
- Sewing thread
- Polystyrene beads to fill

GAUGE (TENSION)
5 sts and 5 rows to 4in (10cm) over st st using US 35 (20mm) needles.

ABBREVIATIONS
See page 124.

PATTERN
Main piece
Use 2 ends throughout, drawing yarn from center and outer of cone.
Using A, cast on 20 sts, leaving a 23½in (60cm) tail.
Row 1: Knit.
Row 2: K12, turn.
Row 3: K10, turn.
Rows 4—9: rep rows 2—3, 3 more times.
Row 10: rep row 2.
Rows 11—20: rep rows 1—10.

Change to B.
Rows 21—30: rep rows 1—10.

Change to A.
Rep rows 1—30, 3 more times.
Bind (cast) off leaving tail of approx. 20in (50cm).

TO MAKE UP
Using a sewing machine, stitch together the two lining pieces with 1cm seam allowance, leaving 4in (10cm) open.

Carefully fill the lining pad with polystyrene beads until it is firm to the touch. Using a

needle and thread, hand stitch the opening closed with small stitches.

Insert the pad into the knitted cover through the open side seam (the cast-on and bound- (cast-) off edges). Lace the seam closed with the tail.

Using yarn tail, gather the top and bottom tightly to close the knitting into a ball. Weave in all loose ends.

Three-tone necklace

AN EVERYDAY NECKLACE IN A SIMPLE AND MODERN DESIGN, THIS IS A FABULOUS
PROJECT FOR USING UP LEFTOVER YARN.

SIZE
Approx. 63in (160cm) x ½in (1.25cm)

MATERIALS
Yarn
Stretchy jersey yarn such as Hoopla Yarn
from Hoopla—100% cotton jersey; approx.
109yds (100m) per 1lb 1½oz (500g) cone.
Weight depends on the fabric the yarn is
made from.
- Light Cyan (A)—approx. 3oz (85g)/
  18½yds (17m)
- Mocha (B)—approx. 1oz (30g)/
  6½yds (6m)
- Deep Blue (C)—approx. 2oz (55g)/
  12yds (11m)

Needles
Two size US 15 (10mm) double pointed
knitting needles.

GAUGE (TENSION)
8 sts and 12 rows to 4in (10cm) over st st
using US 15 (10mm) needles.

ABBREVIATIONS
See page 124.

PATTERN
Main piece
Using A, cast on 2 sts.
Row 1: K2, do not turn. Slide sts to other end
of needle and pull yarn tightly across back
ready to work next row.
Rep row 1 until piece measures 10¼in (26cm).

Change to B.
Rep row 1 until piece measures 19¾in (50cm).

Change to A.
Rep row 1 until piece measures 39½in
(100cm).

Change to C.
Rep row 1 until piece measures 63in (160cm).
Pull yarn end through final 2 sts and pull tight.

TO MAKE UP
Use a sewing needle and thread to stitch the
two ends together to create a loop, ensuring it
isn't twisted.

Wrap yarn over to cover join, thread end in
using tapestry needle and trim excess.

TIP

As this yarn is made from off-cuts from the fashion industry the thickness of each color can be different. If you have one color significantly thinner than the others you could try knitting 2 ends together for that yarn to give a regular overall finish.

Herringbone rug

ADD TEXTURE TO YOUR HOME WITH THIS PERFECT HALLWAY RUG. THE HERRINGBONE STITCH GIVES A LOVELY DENSE KNIT THAT FEELS SOFT UNDERFOOT.

SIZE
Approx. 20½in (52cm) x 44in (112cm)

MATERIALS
Yarn
Stretchy jersey fabric yarn such as Tek Tek from Hoopla—100% cotton jersey; approx. 131yds (120m) per 1lb 5oz (600g) cone. Weight depends on the fabric the yarn is made from.
- Greenish Grey—approx. 4lbs 7oz (2kg)/ 437yds (400m). Quantities are approximate as yarn varies.

Needles
Size US 17 (12mm) circular knitting needle, 31½in (80cm) long

Other materials
- Tapestry needle

GAUGE (TENSION)
11 sts and 9 rows to 4in (10cm) over st st using US 17 (12mm) needles.

ABBREVIATIONS
See page 124.

PATTERN
Main piece
Cast on 50 sts.
Rows 1–6: Knit.
Row 7 (RS): K4, [k2togtbl dropping only the first st off left needle] until 4 sts remain on left needle, k4.
Row 8: K4 [p2tog dropping only the first st off left needle] until 4 sts remain on left needle, k4.
Rep rows 7 and 8, until you have approx. 5oz (150g) of yarn remaining (or the knitting measures approx. 42in (107cm), ending with a row 8.
Next 7 rows: Knit.
Bind (cast) off.

TO MAKE UP
Weave in all loose ends. Steam lightly to shape.

TIP
As the rug will get very heavy it is easiest to knit using a circular needle. You will be able to rest the weight on the wire of the circular needle which will be much gentler on your wrists.

Color-block cardigan

PERFECT OVER A SIMPLE TOP TO ADD COLOR AND TEXTURE TO YOUR OUTFIT,
THIS SLEEVELESS SHAWL-COLLAR CARDIGAN WILL BECOME A SUMMER STAPLE.

SIZE
One size
To fit bust 32—42in (81—107cm)
Length approx. 23½in (60cm)

MATERIALS
Yarn
Stretchy jersey fabric yarn such as Tek Tek from Hoopla—100% cotton jersey; approx. 131yds (120m) per 1lb 5oz (600g) cone. Weight depends on the fabric the yarn is made from.
- Cerise (A)—approx. 15⅞oz (450g)/ 99yds (90m)
- Beige (B)—approx. 9¾oz (275g)/ 60yds (55m)
- Pale Pink (C)—approx. 12¾oz (362g)/ 80yds (72m)

Needles
Pair of size US 19 (15mm) knitting needles

Other materials
- Cable needle
- Tapestry needle

GAUGE (TENSION)
6 sts and 8 rows to 4in (10cm) over st st using US 19 (15mm) needles.

ABBREVIATIONS
See page 124.

PATTERN
Right front
Using A, cast on 40 sts.
Rows 1–6: [K1, p1] to end: (1x1 rib)
Row 7: P4, k4, p4, join in B and [k1, p1] to end.
Twist yarns tog at color change on every row to link sts and prevent holes.
Row 8 and every foll even row until Row 30: [P1, k1] 14 times, change to A, work each st as it presents to end.
Row 9: P4, C4F, p4, change to B, [k1, p1] to end.
Row 11: P3, C3R, C3L, p3, change to B, [k1, p1] to end.
Row 13: P2, C3R, p2, C3L, p2, change to B, [k1, p1] to end.
Row 15: P1, C3R, p4, C3L, p1, change to B, [k1, p1] to end.
Row 17: C3R, p6, C3L, change to B, [k1, p1] to end.
Row 19: C3L, p6, C3R, change to B, [k1, p1] to end.
Row 21: P1, C3L, p4, C3R, p1, change to B, [k1, p1] to end.
Row 23: P2, C3L, p2, C3R, p2, change to B, [k1, p1] to end.
Row 25: P3, C3L, C3R, p3, change to B, [k1, p1] to end.
Row 27: P4, C4F, p4, change to B, [k1, p1] to end.

Row 29: P4, C4F, p4, change to B, [k1, p1] to end.
Row 31: P3, C3R, C3L, p3, change to B, bind (cast) off 10 sts for armhole, p next st, [k1, p1] 8 times.
Row 32: [P1, k1] 9 times, turn knitting, cast on 10 sts, turn knitting, change to A, work each st as it presents to end.

Back

Row 33: P2, C3R, p2, C3L, p2, change to B, [k1, p1] to end.

Row 34: [P1, k1] 14 times, change to A, work each st as it presents to end.

Row 35: P1, C3R, p4, C3L, p1, change to C, k to end.

Row 36 and every foll even row until Row 60: P28, change to A, work each st as it presents to end.

Row 37: C3R, p6, C3L, change to C, k to end.

Row 39: C3L, p6, C3R, change to C, k to end.

Row 41: P1, C3L, p4, C3R, p1, change to C, k to end.

Row 43: P2, C3L, p2, C3R, p2, change to C, k to end.

Row 45: P3, C3L, C3R, p3, change to C, k to end.

Row 47: P4, C4F, p4, change to C, k to end.

Row 49: P4, C4F, p4, change to C, k to end.

Row 51: P3, C3R, C3L, p3, change to C, k to end.

Row 53: P2, C3R, p2, C3L, p2, change to C, k to end.

Row 55: P1, C3R, p4, C3L, p1, change to C, k to end.

Row 57: C3R, p6, C3L, change to C, k to end.

Row 59: C3L, p6, C3R, change to C, k to end.

Row 61: P1, C3L, p4, C3R, p1, change to B, [k1, p1] to end.

Row 62: [P1, k1] 14 times, change to A, work each st as it presents to end.

Row 63: P2, C3L, p2, C3R, p2, change to B, bind (cast) off 10 sts for armhole, p next st, [k1, p1] 8 times.

Row 64: [P1, k1] 9 times, turn knitting, cast on 10 sts, turn knitting, change to A, work each st as it presents to end.

Left front

Row 65: P3, C3L, C3R, p3, change to B, [k1, p1] to end.

Row 66: and every foll even row until Row 88: [P1, k1] 14 times, change to A, work each st as it presents to end.

Row 67: P4, C4F, p4, change to B, [k1, p1] to end.

Row 69: P4, C4F, p4, change to B, [k1, p1] to end.

Row 71: P3, C3R, C3L, p3, change to B, [k1, p1] to end.

Row 73: P2, C3R, p2, C3L, p2, change to B, [k1, p1] to end.

Row 75: P1, C3R, p4, C3L, p1, change to B, [k1, p1] to end.

Row 77: C3R, p6, C3L, change to B, [k1, p1] to end.

Row 79: C3L, p6, C3R, change to B, [k1, p1] to end.

Row 81: P1, C3L, p4, C3R, p1, change to B, [k1, p1] to end.

Row 83: P2, C3L, p2, C3R, p2, change to B, [k1, p1] to end.

Row 85: P3, C3L, C3R, p3, change to B, [k1, p1] to end.

Row 87: P4, C4F, p4, change to B, [k1, p1] to end.

Rows 89–94: [K1, p1] to end. (1x1 rib)
Bind (cast) off.

TO MAKE UP

Weave in all loose ends. Steam lightly to shape.

TIP
Knotting ends of jersey yarn together can cause unsightly lumps. To avoid this, you could use a sewing needle and matching color sewing thread to stitch joins together.

Striped top

IF YOU LOVE CHUNKY KNITS EVEN IN SUMMER, THIS IS THE IDEAL PROJECT FOR YOU.
THE OPEN KNIT STRUCTURE MAKES IT PERFECT FOR WARM DAYS IN THE SUN.

SIZE
To fit bust
S—32–39in (81–99cm)
Length approx. 23¾in (60cm)
M—39–46in (99–117cm)
Length approx. 26¾in (68cm)

MATERIALS
Yarn
Stretchy jersey fabric yarn such as Tek Tek—
100% cotton jersey; approx. 131yds (120m)
per 1lb 5oz (600g) cone. Weight depends on
the fabric the yarn is made from.
- White (A): S—approx. 1lb 5oz (600g)
  131yds (120m); M—approx. 1lb 10oz
  (735g)/160yds (147m). Quantities are
  approximate as yarn varies.
- Turquoise (B): S—approx. 1lb 5oz (600g)/
  131yds (120m); M—approx. 1lb 10oz
  (735g)/160yds (147m). Quantities are
  approximate as yarn varies.

Needles
Size US 15 (10mm) circular knitting needle,
31½in (80cm) long
Size US 17 (12mm) circular knitting needle,
31½in (80cm) long

Other materials
- 2 stitch holders
- Tapestry needle

GAUGE (TENSION)
8 sts and 10 rows to 4in (10cm) over st st
using US 15 (10mm) needles.

ABBREVIATIONS
K1 wy2—knit 1 wrapping yarn twice
around needle
P1 wy2—purl 1 wrapping yarn twice
around needle
See also page 124.

PATTERN
Front and back
Using US 15 (10mm) circular needle and A,
cast on 60 (70) sts.
Rounds 1–6: [K1, p1] to end. (1x1 rib)
Change to US 17 (12mm) circular needle.
Round 7: Purl.
Change to B.
Round 8: Purl.
Change to A.
Round 9: [K1 wy2] to last st, k1.
Change to B.
Round 10: Purl, dropping extra loops.
Change to A.
Round 11: [K1 wy2] to last st, k1
Round 12: Dropping extra loops [K1 wy2] to
last st, k1.
Change to B.
Round 13: Purl, dropping extra loops.
Round 14: Purl.

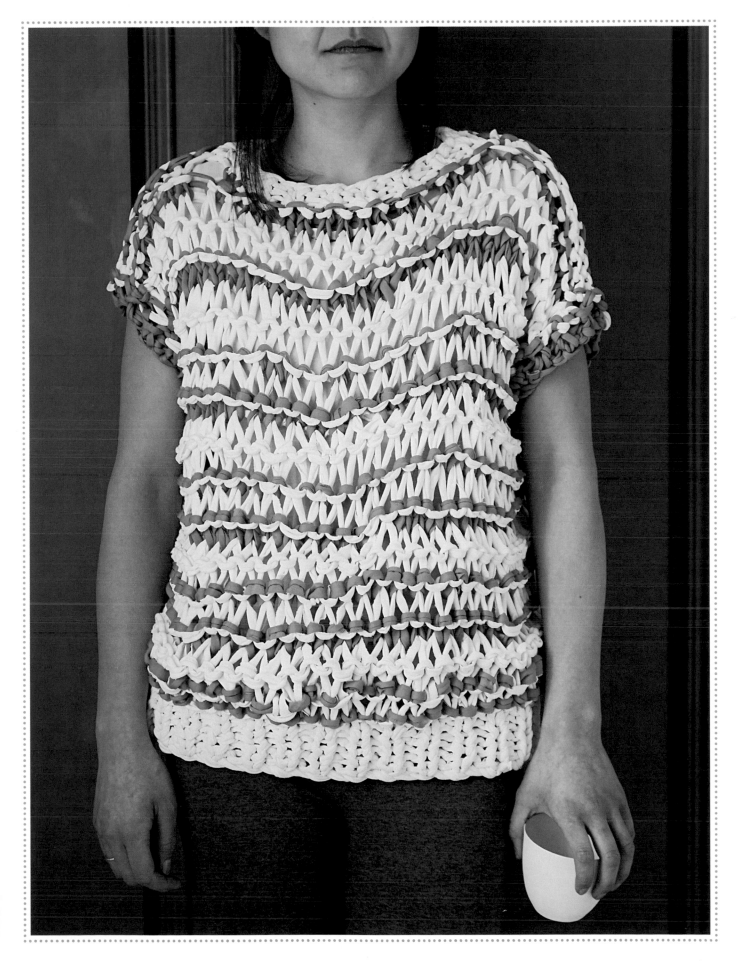

Rounds 15–26: Rep rounds 9–14,
twice more.
Rounds 27–28: Rep rounds 9–10.
Place 30 (35) sts on holder.

Back

Turn knitting and with ws facing work in rows
on 30 (35) sts still on needle.
Change to A.
Row 29: [P1 wy2] to last st, p1.
Row 30: Dropping extra loops [K1 wy2] to last
st, k1.
Change to B.
Row 31: Knit, dropping extra loops.
Row 32: Purl.
Change to A.
Rows 33–36: Rep rows 29–32.

Size M only
Rows 37–40: Rep rows 29–32.

All sizes
Change to A.
Next row: Purl.
Do not bind (cast) off, leave sts on holder to
join at shoulder.

Front

Replace front sts onto US 17 (12mm) circular
knitting needle and with RS facing rejoin
yarn A.
Row 29: [K1 wy2] to last st, k1.
Row 30: Dropping extra loops [P1 wy2] to last
st, p1.
Change to B.
Row 31: Purl, dropping extra loops.
Row 32: Knit.
Rows 33–36: Rep rows 29–32.

Size M only
Rows 37–40: Rep rows 29–32.

All sizes
Change to A.
Next row: Knit.
Do not bind (cast) off, leave the sts on needle
to join at shoulder.

Shoulders

Graft 7 (9) sts at each shoulder using Kitchener
st (see page 119).

Armholes

Using size US 15 (10mm) circular needle and
B, pick up and k 24 (30) sts around armhole.
Round 1: [K1, p1] to end. (1x1 rib)
Bind (cast) off loosely.
Rep for other armhole.

Neck

Transfer 32 (34) sts for neckline from st
holders onto US 15 (10mm) circular needle.
Change to A.
Round 1: [K1, p1] to end. (1x1 rib)
Bind (cast) off loosely.

TO MAKE UP

Weave in all loose ends.

TIP

Try to keep the tension nice
and regular when working in
jersey yarn.

Web tunic

PERFECT FOR THROWING ON OVER A SWIMSUIT, THIS AIRY KNITTED TUNIC MAKES A FABULOUS BEACH OR POOLSIDE COVER UP.

SIZE
To fit bust
S—32–39in (81–99cm)
M—39–46in (99–117cm)
Length approx. 27½in (70cm)

MATERIALS
Yarn
Stretchy jersey fabric yarn such as Tek Tek—100% cotton jersey; approx. 131yds (120m) per 1lb 5oz (600g) cone. Weight depends on the exact fabric the yarn is made from.
• Blue and White pattern: S—1lb 9oz (700g)/153yds (140m); M—1lb 14oz (850g)/186yds (170m). Quantities are approximate as yarn varies.

Needles
Pair of size US 50 (25mm) knitting needles

Other materials
• Tapestry needle

GAUGE (TENSION)
4 sts and 5 rows to 4in (10cm) over st st using US 50 (25mm) needles.

ABBREVIATIONS
K1 wy2—knit 1 wrapping yarn twice around needle
See also page 124.

PATTERN
Front
Cast on 22 (26) sts.
Rows 1–7: Knit.
Row 8 (RS): K1, [K1 wy2] to last st, k1.
Row 9: Knit, dropping extra loops.
Row 10: Knit.
Row 11: Purl.
Row 12: Knit.
Row 13: Purl.
Row 14: K1, [K1 wy2] to last st, k1.
Row 15: Knit, dropping extra loops.
Rows 16–18: Knit.
Rows 19–23: Rep rows 11–15.
Row 24: K10 (11), place worked sts on st holder, bind (cast) off 2 (4), k to end. 10 (11) sts
Row 25: P2tog, p6 (7), p2tog. 8 (9) sts
Row 26: Knit.
Row 27: Purl.
Row 28: K1, [K1 wy2] to last st, k1.
Row 29: Knit, dropping extra loops.
Row 30: K2togtbl, k4 (5), k2tog. 6 (7) sts
Row 31: Knit.
Row 32: K2togtbl, k2 (3), k2tog. 4 (5) sts
Row 33: Knit.
Bind (cast) off.

With WS facing, replace sts from holder onto needle, rejoin yarn and continue working on these sts.
Next row (RS): P2tog, p6 (7), p2tog. 8 (9) sts
Next row: Knit.

TIP
Using larger needles than
a yarn recommends gives the
knitted fabric an airy,
summery feel.

Next row: Purl.
Next row: K1, [K1 wy2] to last st, k1.
Next row: Knit, dropping extra loops.
Next row: K2togtbl, k4 (5), k2tog. 6 (7) sts
Next row: Knit.
Next row: K2togtbl, k2 (3), k2tog. 4 (5) sts
Next row: Knit.
Bind (cast) off.

Back
Cast on 22 (26) sts.
Rows 1–7: Knit.
Row 8 (RS): K1, [K1 wy2] to last st, k1.
Row 9: Knit, dropping extra loops.

Row 10: Knit.
Row 11: Purl.
Row 12: Knit.
Row 13: Purl.
Row 14: K1, [K1 wy2] to last st, k1.
Row 15: Knit, dropping extra loops.
Rows 16–18: Knit.
Rows 19–23: Rep rows 11–15.
Row 24: Knit
Row 25: P2tog, p18 (22), p2tog. 20 (24) sts.
Row 26: Knit.
Row 27: Purl.
Row 28: K1, [K1 wy2] to last st, k1.
Row 29: Knit, dropping extra loops.

Row 30: K2togtbl, k16 (20), k2tog.
18 (22) sts
Row 31: Knit.
Row 32: K2togtbl, k14 (18), k2tog.
16 (20) sts
Row 33: Knit.
Bind (cast) off.

TO MAKE UP
With right sides together join front to back
at shoulder and side seams.

Weave in loose ends.

Jersey yarn bag

THIS HERRINGBONE STITCH BAG WOULD BE PERFECT TO HOLD YOUR KNITTING PROJECTS, BUT ALSO WORKS BRILLIANTLY AS A SUMMER HANDBAG. WOODEN HANDLES MAKE IT IMMENSELY PRACTICAL.

SIZE
12 x 8 in (30.5 x 20cm) not including handles

MATERIALS
Yarn
T-shirt yarn such as Boodles from Hobby Craft—100% Cotton jersey; approx. 99yds (9m) per 1lb (450g) cone. Length depends on the fabric the yarn is made from.
• Turquoise—approx. 1lb (450g)/ 99yds (90m)

Needles
Pair of size US 17 (12mm) knitting needles.
Pair of size US 15 (10mm) knitting needles.

Other materials
• Tapestry needle
• Pair of 10 x 5in (25 x 12cm) wooden handles such as Boodles Wooden Light Handles from Hobbycraft

GAUGE (TENSION)
11 sts and 9 rows to 4in (10cm) over st st using US 17 (12mm) needles.

ABBREVIATIONS
See page 124.

PATTERN
Main piece
Using US 15 (10mm) needles cast on 22 sts.
Row 1: Knit.
Row 2: Purl.
Change to US 17 (12mm) needles.
Row 3: K1tbl, [k2togtbl, dropping only the first st off left needle] to end, k rem st on left needle.
Row 4: K1tbl, [p2tog, dropping only the first st off left needle] to end, k rem st on left needle.
Row 5: Inc 1, [k2togtbl, dropping only the first st off left needle] to end, inc 1 into rem st on left needle. 24 sts
Row 6: K1tbl, [p2tog, dropping only the first st off left needle] to end, k rem st on left needle.
Rows 7—12: Rep rows 5—6, 3 more times. 30 sts
Rows 13—22: Rep rows 3—4, 5 times.
Row 23: K2togtbl, [k2togtbl, dropping only the first st off left needle] to last 2 sts, k2tog. 28 sts
Row 24: K1tbl, [p2tog, dropping only the first st off left needle] to end, k rem st on left needle.
Rows 25—30: Rep rows 23—24, 3 more times. 22 sts
Row 31: K1tbl, [k2togtbl, dropping only the first st off left needle] to end, k rem st on left needle.
Change to US 15 (10mm) needles.
Row 32: K1tbl, [p2tog, dropping only the first st off left needle] to end, k rem st on left needle.
Row 33: Purl.
Row 34: Knit.
Bind (cast) off.

TO MAKE UP

Fold knitting in half so cast-on edge and bound- (cast-) off edge are together. Join side seams, leaving top 2in (5cm) open.

Attach bag handles to top edges using Boodles yarn, by wrapping yarn around the handle, and through the cast-on/bound- (cast-) off edge.

Weave in all loose ends.

TIP
Do not pull the stretchy jersey yarn too tightly as you knit. The herringbone stitch will produce a dense fabric so your knitting tension can remain fairly loose.

Linen scarf

HANDMADE LINEN YARN GIVES THIS SCARF A MODERN LOOK, WHILE THE LADDER STITCH RUNNING THE LENGTH OF THE SCARF LENDS IT A LOVELY LIGHT SUMMERY FEEL.

SIZE
Approx. 8in (20cm) x 63in (160cm)

MATERIALS
Yarn
1in (2.5cm) wide bias-cut handmade yarn, made from linen fabric cut on the bias. See page 123 for cutting instructions.

- White (A)—approx. 8⁷⁄₈oz (250g)/ 55yds (50m), cut from 27½in (70cm) of 53in (135cm) wide fabric. Exact weight will depend on the fabric chosen.
- Pink (B)—approx. 2¾oz (75g)/ 22yds (20m), cut from 19¾in (50cm) of 53in (135cm) wide fabric. Exact weight will depend on the fabric chosen.

Needles
Pair of size US 50 (25mm) knitting needles

Other materials
- Crochet hook (optional)

GAUGE (TENSION)
4 sts and 3½ rows to 4in (10cm) over st st using US 50 (25mm) needles.

ABBREVIATIONS
See page 124.

PATTERN
Main piece
Using A, cast on 10 sts.
Row 1: Knit.
Row 2: Purl.
Row 3: K2, yo, k6, yo, k2. 12 sts
Row 4: Purl.
Rows 5—8: Rep rows 1—2, twice more.
Row 9: K3, C6F, k3.
Row 10: Purl.
Rows 11—16: Rep rows 1—2, 3 more times.
Rep rows 9—16, 3 more times.
Rep rows 9—10.

Change to B.
Rep rows 11—16.
Rep rows 9—16.
Next row: K2, drop st, k6, drop st, k2. 10 sts
Next row: Purl.
Bind (cast) off.

TIP
Keep your knitting nice and loose for this style.

TO FINISH

Pull sides of scarf to run both drop st down the full length.

Weave in all loose ends with your fingers or crochet hook.

Cotton top

TRANSFORM A FLAT PIECE OF COTTON FABRIC INTO A FUNKY SUMMER TOP BY MAKING YOUR OWN YARN AND KNITTING ON BIG NEEDLES.

SIZE

To fit bust
S—32–39in (81–99cm)
Length approx. 22¾in (58cm)
M—39–46in (99–117cm)
Length approx. 26¾in (68cm)

MATERIALS

Yarn

⅜in (1cm) wide handmade yarn, made from cotton fabric. See page 123 for cutting instructions.

- Blue (A)—approx. 10½ oz (300g)/ 131yds (120m), cut from 59in (150cm) of 53in (135cm) wide fabric. Exact weight will depend on the fabric chosen.
- White (B)—approx. 3¼oz (92g)/ 38yds (35m), cut from 30in (76cm) of 53in (135cm) wide fabric. Exact weight will depend on the fabric chosen.

Needles

Pair of size US 35 (20mm) knitting needles

Other materials

- 4 stitch holders
- Tapestry needle
- Crochet hook (optional)

GAUGE (TENSION)

5 sts and 6 rows to 4in (10cm) over st st using US 35 (20mm) needles.

ABBREVIATIONS

See page 124.

PATTERN

Front

Using A, cast on 28 (34) sts.
Row 1: K1, [yo, skpo] to last st, k1.
Row 2: Purl.
Rows 3–14: Rep rows 1–2, 6 more times.
Row 15: Bind (cast) off 2 sts, [yo, skpo] to last st, k1. 26 (32) sts
Row 16: Bind (cast) off 2 sts, p to end. 24 (30) sts
Rows 17–22: Rep rows 1–2, three more times.

Size M only

Rep rows 1–2, 3 more times.

All sizes

Change to B.
Next row: Purl.
Next row: Knit.
Next row: P10 (12), turn. Place remaining sts on stitch holder 1.

TIP
Choose a fabric which doesn't have too much of a contrast in color between the back and the front of the cloth to avoid the garment looking too spotty.

Next row: Knit.
Next row: P7 (9), p2tog, p1. 9 (11) sts
Next row: Knit.
Next row: P6 (8), p2tog, p1. 8 (10) sts
Next row: Knit.
Next row: P5 (7), p2tog, p1. 7 (9) sts
Next row: Knit.
Place remaining sts on stitch holder 2.

Place sts from stitch holder 1 back on needle and rejoin yarn at center front.
Bind (cast) off 4 (6) sts, p to end. 10 (12) sts
Next row: Knit.
Next row: P1, p2tog, p to end. 9 (11) sts
Rep these 2 rows, twice more.
Next row: Knit.
Place remaining sts on stitch holder 1.

Back
Using A, cast on 28 (34) sts.
Work as front to row 22.

Size M only
Rep rows 1—2, 3 more times.

All sizes
Change to B.
Next row: Purl.
Next row: Knit.
Next row: Purl.
Next row: Knit.
Next row: P 9 (11), turn. Place remaining sts on stitch holder 3.
Next row: Knit.
Next row: P6 (8), p2tog, p1. 8 (10) sts
Next row: Knit.
Next row: P5 (7), p2tog, p1. 7 (9) sts
Next row: Knit.

Place remaining sts on stitch holder 4.
Place sts from stitch holder 3 back on needle and rejoin yarn at center back.
Bind (cast) off 6 (8) sts, p to end. 9 (11) sts
Next row: Knit.
Next row: P1, p2tog, p to end. 8 (10) sts
Rep these 2 rows, once more. 7 (9) sts
Next row: Knit.
Leave sts on needle.

TO FINISH
Graft seams at shoulders using Kitchener stitch (see page 119) in self yarn.

With right sides together join front to back at side seams.

Weave in all loose ends.

Linen shrug

THIS VERSATILE SHRUG IS INCREDIBLY SIMPLE TO KNIT, AND PERFECT AS A SUMMER LAYER OVER A SLEEVELESS TOP TO PROTECT YOUR SHOULDERS.

SIZE
Approx. 29½in (75cm) wide x 24¾in (63cm) long

MATERIALS
Yarn
⅜in (1cm) wide bias-cut handmade yarn, made from linen fabric cut on the bias. See page 123 for cutting instructions.
- Lime—approx. 19½oz (550g)/ 110yds (100m), cut from 59in (150cm) of 53in (135cm) wide fabric. Exact weight will depend on the fabric chosen.

Needles
Pair of size US 19 (15mm) knitting needles

Other materials
- Tapestry needle
- Crochet hook (optional)

GAUGE (TENSION)
4½ sts and 6 rows to 4in (10cm) over st st using US 19 (15mm) needles.

ABBREVIATIONS
See page 124.

PATTERN
Main piece
Cast on 34 sts.
Rows 1—4: [K1, p1] to end. (1x1 rib)
Row 5: Knit.
Row 6: Purl.
Rows 7—34: Rep rows 5—6, 14 more times.
Rows 35—38: Rep rows 1—4.
Bind (cast) off.

TO FINISH
Fold the finished knitting in half widthwise with right sides together, aligning the cast-on and bound- (cast-) off edges.

Stitch side edges closed for 6 rows from cast-on and bound- (cast-) off edges.

Weave in all loose ends with your fingers or a crochet hook.

TIP
For a winter version of this simple shrug, try substituting a wool yarn suitable for US 19 (15mm) knitting needles.

CHAPTER 3

Mega Knits

Step it up a notch in this final selection of projects with the biggest of the big knits. Watch your knitting grow at an amazing speed when using the largest needles and super-thick yarn, then immerse yourself in the soft and snuggly finished projects to keep the winter chills firmly at bay.

Chunky hat

THIS MEGA CHUNKY HAT MUST BE THE ULTIMATE IN WINTERWEAR, AND THE LOOK OF IT CAN EASILY BE CHANGED BY USING A PLAIN OR A VARIEGATED YARN, AS SEEN ON PAGE 125. EVERYONE IN YOUR FAMILY WILL WANT ONE.

SIZE

Approx. 10¼in (26cm) high, with brim rolled up, and 18in (46cm) circumference, stretching to 22in (56cm) circumference

MATERIALS

Yarn

Super chunky yarn designed to be knitted on size US 50 (25mm) needles, such as Fat Bubba by Melanie Porter—100% British Wool; approx. 39½yds (36m) per 8⅞oz (250g) ball; or Big Loop Yarn from Loopy Mango—100% Merino Wool; approx. 120yds (115m) per 40oz (1134g) skein

- Green hat—Fat Bubba: Apple Green—6oz (170g)/27yds (25m)
- Gray hat—Big Loop Yarn: Ash—8½oz (240g)/26yds (24.5m)

Needles

Size US 50 (25mm) circular knitting needle, 23½in (60cm) long

Other materials

- Tapestry needle

GAUGE (TENSION)

4 sts and 5 rows to 4in (10cm) over st st using US 50 (25mm) needles.

ABBREVIATIONS

See page 124.

PATTERN

Main piece

Cast on 18 sts using thumb method (see page 109).
Knit in the round.
Rounds 1–11: Knit.
Round 12: [K2tog, K4] to end. 15 sts
Round 13 (and all following odd rounds): Knit.
Round 14: [K2tog, K3] to end. 12 sts
Round 16: [K2tog, K2] to end. 9 sts
Round 18: [K2tog, K1] to end. 6 sts
Run 6in (15cm) of yarn through the 6 sts on needle and pull tight.
Secure end.

TO MAKE UP

Weave in all loose ends. Steam lightly to shape.

Supersized scarf

THE GENEROUS SIZE OF THIS SHAWL/SCARF MAKES IT THE ULTIMATE COZY FASHION ACCESSORY.

SIZE
Approx. 17¾in (45cm) x 91in (230cm)

MATERIALS
Yarn
Super chunky yarn designed to be knitted on size US 50 (25mm) needles, such as Fat Bubba by Melanie Porter——100% British Wool; approx. 82yds (75m) per 17½oz (500g) ball.
• Amber——35oz (1kg)/164yds (150m)

Needles
Pair of size US 50 (25mm) knitting needles

Other materials
• Tapestry needle or crochet hook to weave in ends

GAUGE (TENSION)
4 sts and 5 rows to 4in (10cm) over st st using US 50 (25mm) needles

ABBREVIATIONS
See page 124.

PATTERN
Main piece
Cast on 16 sts.
Row 1: Knit.
Rows 2–3: Purl.
Row 4: Knit.
Rows 5–8: Rep rows 1–4.
Row 9: Knit.
Row 10: Purl.
Rep rows 9–10 until you have approx. 3½oz (100g) yarn remaining, finishing with a knit row.
Rep rows 1–8.
Bind (cast) off purlwise.

TO MAKE UP
Weave in all loose ends. Steam lightly to shape.

TIP
If you would like to make the shawl even bigger, you could use exactly the same pattern on custom-made 1½in (35mm) needles.

Infinity scarf

LIGHTWEIGHT YET SUPER SOFT, WRAP THIS INFINITY SCARF AROUND TWICE
FOR COMPLETE WINTER WEATHER PROTECTION.

SIZE

Custom-made 1½in (35mm) needles:
approx. 8in (20cm) wide and 50½in (128cm)
circumference **or** US 50 (25mm) needles:
approx. 7⅛in (18cm) wide and 47¼in (120cm)
circumference.

MATERIALS

Yarn

Mega chunky yarn such as Quickie from Lion
Brand—74% acrylic, 22% wool, 4%
polyester; 22yds (20m) per 3oz (85g) ball.
• Spicy—approx. 6oz (170g)/44yds (40m)

Needles

Pair of custom-made size 1½in (35mm) **or**
size US 50 (25mm) knitting needles.

Other materials

• Tapestry needle

GAUGE (TENSION)

3 sts and 3 rows to 4in (10cm) over st st using
1½in (35mm) needles **or** 3 sts and 4 rows to
4in (10cm) over st st using US 50 (25mm)
needles.

ABBREVIATIONS

See page 124.

PATTERN

Main piece

Cast on 7 sts.
Row 1: Knit.
Row 2: Purl.
Rep rows 1–2, until you have approx. 20in
(50cm) of yarn remaining.
Bind (cast) off.

TO MAKE UP

Secure cast-on edge to bound- (cast-) off edge
using mattress st (see page 119), ensuring
that the scarf is not twisted.

Weave in loose ends and steam lightly
to shape.

TIP

I have used custom-made
1½in (35mm) needles to get an even
larger and loftier knit. This pattern will work
equally well on US 50 (25mm) needles
(measurements also given left).

Cable floor pillow

INTRODUCE TEXTURE AND COMFORT INTO YOUR HOME WITH THIS LARGE STATEMENT PILLOW, MADE IN A FABULOUS NATURAL-COLORED MEGA BULKY ALPACA YARN.

SIZE
Approx. 29½in (75cm) square

MATERIALS
Yarn
Super chunky yarn, designed to be knitted on size US 50 (25mm) needles, such as Big Stitch Alpaca from Bagsmith, 67% alpaca, 27% wool, 6% nylon; approx. 125yds (115m) per 40oz (1.13kg) "bump."
• Multi fawn—35¼oz (1kg)/110yds (100m)

Needles
Size US 50 (25mm) circular knitting needle, 23½in (60cm) long (or longer)

Other materials
• Cable needle
• Pillow form measuring 29½in (75cm) square
• 2 pieces backing fabric, each measuring 30in (76cm) square
• Sewing needle and matching sewing thread

GAUGE (TENSION)
2½ sts and 4 rows to 4in (10cm) over st st using US 50 (25mm) needles.

ABBREVIATIONS
See page 124.

PATTERN
Main piece
Cast on 20 sts.
Row 1: P5, k6, p9.
Row 2 and every following even row: K9, p6, k5.
Row 3: P5, k6, p9.
Row 5: P5, k6, p9.
Row 7: P5, C6F, p9.
Row 9: P5, k6, p9.
Row 10: K9, p6, k5.
Rep rows 1–10, twice more.
Rep rows 1–2.
Bind (cast) off.

TIP

As the stitches are so large it
is possible to see the pillow form
through the knitting. To avoid this
I suggest using a complementary color
fabric layer under the knit.

TO MAKE UP

Weave in all loose ends. Steam lightly
to shape.

Pin the two pieces of backing fabric with right
sides together, and sew around 3 sides with
⅜in (1cm) seam allowance.

Turn cover through to right side out and insert
pillow form.

Hand stitch final side closed with slipstitch,
turning raw edges under as you stitch.

Hand stitch knit panel around 4 sides to cover
front of pillow.

Cable poncho

COZY UP IN THIS INDULGENT CHUNKY KNIT PONCHO WITH CABLE AND RIB DETAILS.
PERFECT TO WEAR OUT ON A CHILLY DAY, OR FOR LOUNGING AROUND AT HOME.

SIZE
Approx. length 28½in (72cm); approx.
width across back 25½in (65cm)

MATERIALS
Yarn
Super chunky yarn, designed to be knitted
on size US 50 (25mm) needles, such as
Fat Bubba by Melanie Porter——100%
British Wool; approx. 82yds (75m) per
17½oz (500g) ball.
• Soft White——35oz (1kg)/
  164yds (150m)

Needles
Size US 50 (25mm) circular knitting
needle, 23½in (60cm) long

Other materials
• Cable needle
• Tapestry needle

GAUGE (TENSION)
4 sts and 5 rows to 4in (10cm) over st st
using US 50 (25mm) needles

ABBREVIATIONS
See page 124.

PATTERN
Main piece, worked in rows.
Cast on 18 sts.
Row 1 (RS): P6, k4, p6, k1, p1.
Row 2: K1, p1, k6, p4, k6.
Row 3: P5, C3R, C3L, p5, k1, p1.
Row 4 and every following even row: Work
every st as it presents.
Row 5: P4, C3R, p2, C3L, p4, k1, p1.
Row 7: P3, C3R, C4F, C3L, p3, k1, p1.
Row 9: P2, C3R, p1, k4, p1, C3L, p2, k1, p1.
Row 11: P1, C3R, p2, C4F, p2, C3L, p1, k1, p1.
Row 13: P1, k2, p3, k4, p3, k2, p1, k1, p1.
Row 15: P1, C3L, p2, C4F, p2, C3R, p1, k1, p1.
Row 17: P2, C3L, p1, k4, p1, C3R, p2, k1, p1.
Row 19: P3, C3L, C4F, C3R, p3, k1, p1.
Row 21: P4, C3L, p2, C3R, p4, k1, p1.
Row 23: P5, C3L, C3R, p5, k1, p1.
Row 25: P6, C4F, p6, k1, p1.
Row 26: Work every st as it presents.
Rep rows 3—26.
Rep rows 3—24.
Bind (cast) off.

Pick up and k 22 sts from center 26 rows
along right-hand edge and work at 90 degrees
to knitting.
Row 1: P2, [k2, p2] to end.
Row 2: K2, [p2, k2] to end.
Rows 3—12: Rep rows 1—2, 5 more times.
Row 13: Rep row 1.
Bind (cast) off.

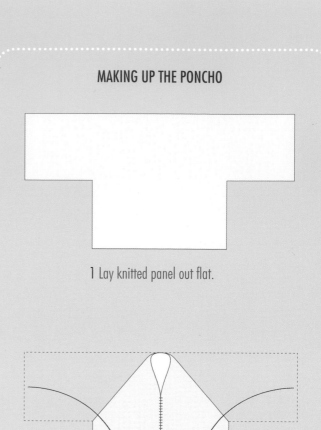

MAKING UP THE PONCHO

1 Lay knitted panel out flat.

2 Fold over both sides, and join center and side seams.

TO MAKE UP

Fold knitting as shown in diagram (above right) and stitch center front and side seams leaving approx. 7in (18cm) open for armholes and approx. 24in (61cm) open for neck.

Weave in all loose ends. Steam lightly to shape.

TIP
For a seamless join in the
yarn use a felting needle to
join ends.

Cable scarf

KEEP ON-TREND AND COZY IN EVEN THE COLDEST WEATHER WITH THIS MEGA CHUNKY SCARF. CABLES LOOK THEIR BEST IN CHUNKY YARNS, AND THIS STYLE TAKES IT TO THE EXTREME!

SIZE
Approx. 8¾in (22cm) x 59¾in (152cm)

MATERIALS
Yarn
Super chunky yarn, designed to be knitted on size US 50 (25mm) needles, such as Fat Bubba by Melanie Porter—100% British Wool; approx. 82yds (75m) per 17½oz (500g) ball.
• Hot Pink—17½oz (500g)/82yds (75m)

Needles
Pair of size US 50 (25mm) knitting needles

Other materials
• Cable needle
• Tapestry needle

GAUGE (TENSION)
4 sts and 5 rows to 4in (10cm) over st st using US 50 (25mm) needles

ABBREVIATIONS
See page 124.

PATTERN
Main piece
Cast on 10 sts.
Row 1: P2, k6, p2.
Row 2: K2, p6, k2.
Rows 3—8: Rep rows 1—2, 3 more times.
Row 9: P2, C6F, p2.
Row 10: K2, p6, k2.
Rep rows 1—10, 6 more times.
Rep rows 1—8.
Bind (cast) off.

TO MAKE UP
Weave in all loose ends. Steam lightly to shape.

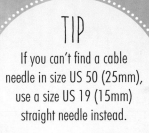

TIP
If you can't find a cable
needle in size US 50 (25mm),
use a size US 19 (15mm)
straight needle instead.

TIP

I recommend using circular needles instead of straight ones as it is easier to work this number of stitches along the wire, rather than pushed onto one needle.

Two-tone jacket

WORKED IN A LOVELY TEXTURED MOSS STITCH THIS CHUNKY JACKET IS EASY TO KNIT AND FUN TO WEAR. USING TWO CONTRAST COLOR YARNS KNITTED TOGETHER ADDS TO ITS RUSTIC FEEL.

SIZE

Approx. length 21½in (55cm); approx. width across back 22in (56cm); approx. sleeve length 9in (23cm)

MATERIALS

Yarn

Super chunky yarn designed to be knitted on size US 15 (10mm) or US 17 (12mm) needles, such as Magnum from Cascade— 100% Peruvian Wool; approx. 123yds/112m per 8⅞oz (250g) ball.

• Ecru—17¾oz (500g)/246yds (224m)
• Walnut Heather—17¾oz (500g)/ 246yds (224m)

Needles

Size US 50 (25mm) circular knitting needle.

Other materials

• Stitch holder
• Tapestry needle

GAUGE (TENSION)

Work 2 ends together
3½ sts and 6 rows to 4in (10cm) over moss st using US 50 (25mm) needles.

ABBREVIATIONS

See page 124.

PATTERN

Back

Cast on 20 sts.
Row 1: [K1, p1] to end.
Row 2: [P1, k1] to end. (Moss st)
Rows 3–34: Rep rows 1–2, 16 more times.
Do not bind (cast) off.

Front

Row 35: [K1, p1] 5 times. Place remaining 10 sts onto stitch holder and turn work to continue working on sts on needle.
Row 36: Rep row 2.
Rows 37–68: Rep rows 1–2, 16 times.
Bind (cast) off.

Return sts on stitch holder to needle. Turn work to start knitting at the side seam.
Rows 35–68: Rep rows 1–2, 17 times.
Bind (cast) off.

Sleeves

Pick up and k 16 sts over central 17¼in (44cm) along right-hand edge. Work at 90 degrees to main piece.
Row 1: [K1, p1] to end.
Row 2: [P1, k1] to end.
Rows 3–14: Rep rows 1–2, 6 more times.
Bind (cast) off.

Rep on left-hand edge for left sleeve.

TO MAKE UP

Join side and underarm seams.

Weave in loose ends and steam lightly to shape.

Chunky bramble throw

KNIT A MEGA CHUNKY THROW IN SUPER QUICK TIME WITH THIS FABULOUSLY THICK YARN AND BIG NEEDLES. PLACE ON A BED OR COUCH FOR A CONTEMPORARY HOME ACCESSORY.

SIZE

Custom-made 1½in (35mm) needles: approx. 35½in (90cm) x 51in (130cm) **or** US 50 (25mm) needles: approx. 32in (81cm) x 43in (109cm)

MATERIALS

Yarn

Mega chunky yarn such as Quickie from Lion Brand——74% acrylic, 22% wool, 4% polyester; approx. 22yds (20m) per 3oz (85g) ball.

• Icy——1lb 14oz (850g)/220yds (200m)

Needles

Pair of custom-made size 1½ in (35mm) **or** size US 50 (25mm) knitting needles

GAUGE (TENSION)

3 sts and 3 rows to 4in (10cm) over st st using 1½in (35mm) needles **or** 3 sts and 4 rows to 4in (10cm) over st st using US 50 (25mm) needles.

ABBREVIATIONS

See page 124.

PATTERN

Main piece

Cast on 34 sts.

Row 1 and following odd rows: Purl.

Row 2: K1, *p3tog, [k1, p1, k1] all into next st*; rep from * to * to last st, k1.

Row 4: K1, *[k1, p1, k1] all into next st, p3tog*; rep from * to * to last st, k1.

Rep these 4 rows until approx. half a ball of yarn remains and blanket measures approx. 50in (127cm) long, ending with a purl row.

Bind (cast) off.

TO MAKE UP

Weave in all loose ends. Steam lightly to shape.

TIP

This yarn is best knitted with a loose tension.

Body warmer

A FABULOUS LAYER IN A BIG STATEMENT KNIT. WITHOUT BULKY SLEEVES, YOU CAN EASILY WEAR THIS COZY GILET UNDER A COAT.

SIZE
To fit bust
S—32–39in (81–99cm)
Length approx. 23½ in (60cm)
M—39–46in (99–117cm)
Length approx. 27½ in (70cm)

MATERIALS
Yarn
Mega chunky yarn such as Quickie from Lion Brand—74% acrylic, 22% wool, 4% polyester; 22yds (20m) per 3oz (85g) ball.
- Peppery: S—approx. 15oz (425g)/ 110yds (100m); M—approx. 1lb 8oz (680g) /176yds (160m)

Needles
Size US 50 (25mm) circular knitting needle, 47in (120cm) long
Size US 50 (25mm) circular knitting needle, 23½in (60cm) long

Other materials
- 3 stitch holders
- Tapestry needle

GAUGE (TENSION)
3 sts and 4 rows to 4in (10cm) over st st using US 50 (25mm) needles.

ABBREVIATIONS
See page 124.

PATTERN
Back and front
Using the longer circular needle, cast on 26 (30) sts loosely with the thumb method (see page 109).
Round 1: [Yo, k2, pass yo over k2] to end.
Rounds 2 and 4: Knit.
Round 3: K1, [yo, k2, pass yo over k2] to last st, k1.
Rounds 5–12: Rep rounds 1–4, twice more.
Round 13: [Yo, k2, pass yo over k2] to end.
Round 14: Knit.
Round 15: K1, [yo, k2, pass yo over k2] to last st, k1.

Size M only
Rep rounds 12–15.

All sizes
Place 13 (15) sts onto stitch holder 1.

Back
Turn knitting and work in rows on 13 (15) sts still on needle.
Next row: P13 (15).
Next row: K1 [yo, k2, pass yo over k2] to end.
Next row: P13 (15).
Next row: [Yo, k2, pass yo over k2] to last st, k1.

TIP

If you love this stitch, but would like to make it into a sweater, follow the instructions for the sleeves on the Two-tone jacket on page 93.

Next row: P13 (5).
Next row: K1 [yo, k2, pass yo over k2] to end.
Next row: P13 (5).
Do not bind off, place sts on stitch holder 2.

Front

Place sts from stitch holder 1 back on needle and rejoin yarn on front, with ws facing on right-hand needle. Work in rows.
Next row: P13 (15).
Next row: [Yo, k2, pass yo over k2] to last st, k1.
Next row: P5, bind (cast) off 3 (5) sts purlwise, p to end.
Next row: K1, [yo, k2, pass yo over k2] twice. Place first 5 sts worked in row before last on stitch holder 3.

Next row: P2tog, p3. 4 sts.
Next row: [Yo, k2, pass yo over k2] twice.
Next row: p2tog, p2. 3 sts.
Do not bind (cast) off, place sts on stitch holder 1.

Place sts from stitch holder 3 back on needle and rejoin yarn, to work on right front sts, with rs facing.
Next row: K1, [yo, k2, pass yo over k2] twice.
Next row: P3, p2tog. 4 sts.
Next row: K1, [yo, k2, pass yo over k2], k1.
Next row: P2, p2tog. 3 sts.
Do not bind (cast) off, place sts on stitch holder 3.

Shoulders

Graft 3 sts at each shoulder using Kitchener st (see page 119).

Neck

With right side facing out, place sts from stitch holder 2 onto the shorter circular needle, then pick up and k 13 (15) sts from front neckline. 20 (24) sts
Rows 1–3: Knit.
Bind (cast) off loosely.

TO MAKE UP

Weave in all loose ends.

Chunky sweater

GREAT WORN WITH LEGGINGS OR SLIM FIT JEANS, THIS MEGA KNIT SWEATER IS A REAL FASHION STATEMENT. THE AIRY YARN MEANS THAT ALTHOUGH IT IS LOVELY AND CHUNKY, IT ISN'T TOO BULKY TO WEAR.

SIZE
To fit bust
S—32–39in (81–99cm)
Length approx. 25½in (65cm)
M—39–46in (99–117cm)
Length approx. 29½in (75cm)

MATERIALS
Yarn
Mega chunky yarn such as Quickie from Lion Brand—74% acrylic, 22% wool, 4% polyester; 22yds (20m) per 3oz (85g) ball.
• Salty: S—approx. 1lb 9oz (700g)/ 183yds (168m); M—approx. 2lbs 4oz (1.02kg)/264yds (240m)

Needles
Size US 50 (25mm) circular knitting needle, 47in (120cm) long
Size US 50 (25mm) circular knitting needle, 23½ in (60cm) long

Other materials
• 3 stitch holders
• Tapestry needle

GAUGE (TENSION)
3 sts and 4 rows to 4in (10cm) over st st using US 50 (25mm) needles.

ABBREVIATIONS
See page 124.

PATTERN
Back and front
Using the longer circular needle, cast on 30 (34) sts loosely with the thumb method (see page 109).

Rounds 1–2: [K1, p1] to end. (1x1 rib)
Rounds 3–20: Knit.

Size M only
Rep rounds 3–4.

All sizes
Place 15 (17) sts onto stitch holder 1.

Back
Turn knitting and work in rows on sts still on needle.
Next row: Purl.
Next row: Knit.
Rep last 2 rows, twice more.

Size M only
Rep last 2 rows.

All sizes
Do not bind (cast) off, place sts on stitch holder 2. Cut yarn leaving 6in (15cm) tail.

Front
Place sts from stitch holder 1 back on needle and rejoin yarn on front, with rs facing. Work in rows.
Next row: Knit.
Next row: Purl.

Size M only
Rep last 2 rows.

All sizes
Next row: K6, bind (cast) off 3 (5) sts, k to end.
Next row: P4, p2tog. 5 sts.
Place first set of 6 sts on stitch holder 1.
Next row: K2togtbl, k3. 4 sts.
Next row: P4.
Do not bind (cast) off, leave sts on stitch holder 3. Cut yarn leaving 6in (15cm) tail.

Place sts from stitch holder 1 back on needle and rejoin yarn, to work on left front sts, with rs facing.
Next row: K4, k2tog. 5 sts.
Next row: P2tog, p3. 4 sts.
Next row: K4.
Do not bind (cast) off, place sts on stitch holder 1. Cut yarn leaving 6in (15cm) tail.

Shoulders
Graft 4 sts at each shoulder using Kitchener st (see page 119).

Neck
With right side facing out, place sts from stitch holder 2 onto the shorter circular needle, then pick up and k 12 (14) sts from front neckline.
Rounds 1–8: Knit.
Bind (cast) off loosely.

Sleeves
Using the shorter circular needle, pick up and k 12 (14) sts around right armhole.
Rounds 1–16: Knit.
Rounds 17–19: [K1, p1] to end. (1x1 rib)
Bind (cast) off loosely.
Repeat for left sleeve.

TO MAKE UP
Weave in all loose ends.

TIP
Work this sweater seamless to prevent bulky seams.

CHAPTER 4

Equipment & Techniques

Get yourself set up for knitting perfect projects with all of the invaluable help and information in this section. Find out about different needles, learn the basic stitches and the best way to finish and make up your creations, as well as how to substitute different yarns for the projects.

Basic knitting equipment

THE PROJECTS IN THIS BOOK REQUIRE ONLY THE SIMPLEST TOOLS TO MAKE THEM.

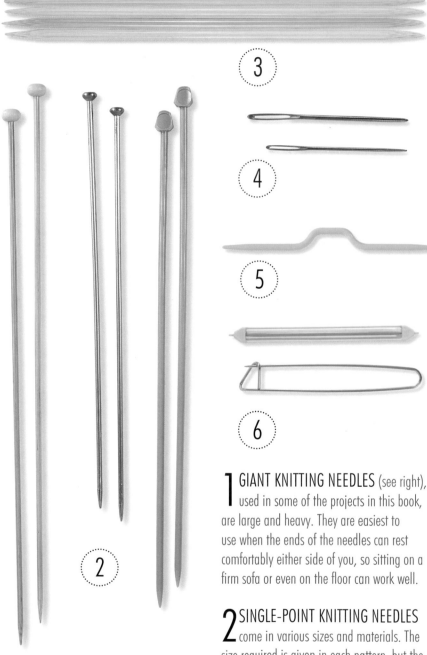

3 DOUBLE-POINTED KNITTING NEEDLES (DPNS) are used in sets of four or five (sets of four are fine for the projects in this book) and allow you to knit off both ends in order to knit in the round (see page 118). You can also use just two DPNs to create a thin tube of knitting (often called i-cord), as for the necklace on page 50.

4 TAPESTRY NEEDLE is used to sew together pieces of knitting (see page 119). These needles have blunt ends to help prevent them splitting the yarn.

5 CABLE NEEDLE is used to hold a group of stitches at the front or back of the work while working a cable twist (see page 117). The size should correspond with the size of knitting needles being used. You can get cranked cable needles, like this one, which are easier to use than straight cable needles if you are a beginner knitter.

6 STITCH HOLDERS These are clips with a horizontal bar that you slip groups of stitches onto, and then clip closed, in order to save the stitches for later use.

1 GIANT KNITTING NEEDLES (see right), used in some of the projects in this book, are large and heavy. They are easiest to use when the ends of the needles can rest comfortably either side of you, so sitting on a firm sofa or even on the floor can work well.

2 SINGLE-POINT KNITTING NEEDLES come in various sizes and materials. The size required is given in each pattern, but the material is a personal choice for the knitter. Beginners often find bamboo needles easiest because they are less slippery than metal or plastic knitting needles.

Knitting techniques

FOR BEGINNER KNITTERS THE FOLLOWING PAGES WILL SHOW YOU ALL THE TECHNIQUES YOU NEED TO GET YOU STARTED WITH THE SIMPLER PROJECTS IN THIS BOOK. MASTER HOW TO CAST ON, FORM KNIT AND PURL STITCHES, AND BIND (CAST) OFF, BEFORE MOVING ONTO CABLING AND SHAPING (THEY ARE EASIER THAN YOU MIGHT THINK ONCE YOU'RE FAMILIAR WITH THE BASICS).

HOLDING NEEDLES AND YARN

Every knitter will develop their own style, but there are two popular ways to hold the knitting needles. Try them both and adopt the style that feels more natural for you.

Holding the yarn

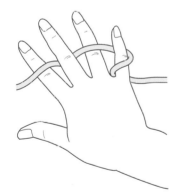

In order to create even knitting the yarn will need to be tensioned. You can wrap the yarn differently around your fingers depending on your natural gauge (tension), but try this method first because it works for most people.

Wind the yarn around your little finger and lace it over the ring finger, under the second finger and over the first finger. The right-hand index finger will be used to wind the yarn around the needle point.

Right hand like a knife

Pick up the needles in both hands as you would a knife and fork, with the needles running under the palms of your hands. You will need to let go of the knitting with your right hand——tuck the blunt end of the needle under your arm to hold it——in order to move the yarn around the tip of the needle.

Right hand like a pen

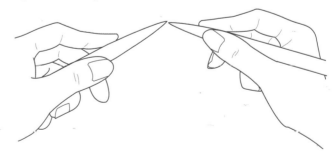

Keeping the left hand in the same position, hold the right-hand needle as you would hold a pen, with the needle resting in the crook of your hand. This position has the advantage that you can control the yarn with your right index finger without letting go of the needles.

SLIP KNOT

Every piece of knitting starts with a simple slip knot.

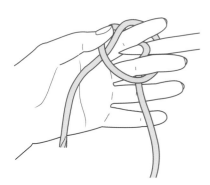

1 Leaving about a 4in (10cm) tail, wind the yarn twice around two fingers of your left hand. Slip the tip of a knitting needle between your fore and second fingers and under the loop furthest from the fingertips, as shown. Draw this loop through the other loop.

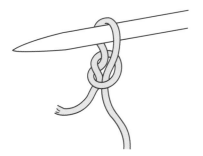

2 Pull on the ends of the yarn to tighten the loop on the needle; this has created the first stitch.

CASTING ON (CABLE METHOD)

I usually use the cable method to cast on stitches: this technique can be used in most projects in this book and creates a neat, firm edge.

1 Hold needle with slip knot in your left hand. Insert the tip of the right-hand needle from left to right into the front of the knot.

3 Draw the yarn through to form a new stitch on the right-hand needle.

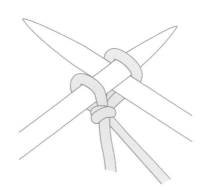

5 For every following stitch, insert the right-hand needle between the two previous stitches.

2 *Wrap the yarn under and around the tip of the right-hand needle.

4 Slip this stitch from the right-hand needle onto the left-hand needle.

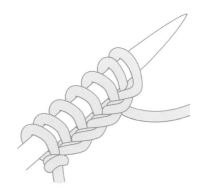

6 Repeat from * until you have the required number of stitches on the left-hand needle.

Extra stitches To cast on extra stitches in the middle of a project, repeat from step 5.

CASTING ON (THUMB METHOD)
Here is an alternative method of casting on.

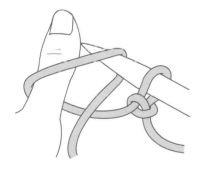 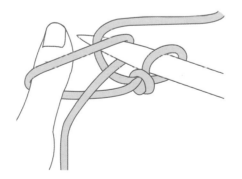 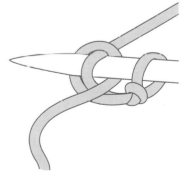

1 Make a slip knot, leaving a tail of yarn approximately four times longer than the width of the total stitches to be cast on. Wrap the tail of yarn around the left thumb from front to back to make a loop, holding the yarn between the fingers of the left hand to keep it taut. Insert the needle through the yarn loop on the thumb.

2 Now bring the yarn from the ball or skein between the left thumb and needle, and take it around the needle.

3 Bring the yarn on the needle through the loop made by the thumb, and pull on both ends of yarn gently to complete the stitch on the needle. Repeat until the desired number of stitches have been cast on.

KNIT STITCH

This is the first and easiest stitch that a beginner will learn. Rows of knit stitches create garter stitch. The yarn should be held at the back of the work.

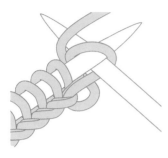

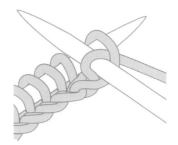

1 Hold the needle with the cast-on stitches in your left hand. Insert the right-hand needle into the front of the first stitch, from left to right (this is called "knitwise"), and take the yarn under and around the tip.

2 Use the tip of the right-hand needle to draw the loop through the stitch.

3 Slip the original stitch off the left-hand needle to complete the first knit stitch. Repeat these three steps until all the stitches on the left-hand needle have been transferred to the right-hand needle. At the end of the row, swap the needles so that all the stitches are again in your left hand.

CONTINENTAL STYLE: KNIT STITCH

An alternative way of knitting is to hold the yarn in your left hand in the style known as Continental. This is how you make a knit stitch using this method.

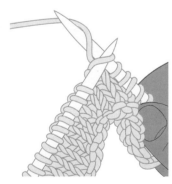

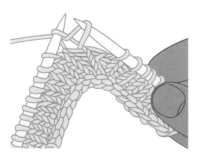

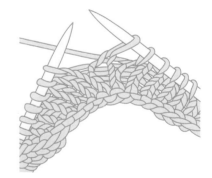

1 Hold the needle with the stitches to be knitted in your left hand. Insert the tip of the right-hand needle into the front of the first stitch from left to right. Holding the yarn fairly taut with your left hand at the back of your work, use the tip of the right-hand needle to pick up a loop of yarn.

2 With the tip of the right-hand needle, bring the yarn through the original stitch to form a loop. This loop will be your new stitch.

3 Slip the original stitch off the left-hand needle by gently pulling the right-hand needle to the right.
  Repeat these three steps until all the stitches on the left-hand needle have been transferred to the right-hand needle. At the end of the row, swap the needles so that all the stitches are again in your left hand.

PURL STITCH

This is the only other basic stitch to master. A row of knit stitch followed by a row of purl stitch creates stockinette (stocking) stitch. The yarn should be held at the front of the work.

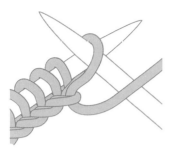  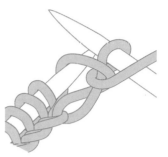

1 Hold the needle with the cast-on stitches in your left hand. Insert the right-hand needle into the front of the first stitch, from right to left (this is called "purlwise").

2 Take the yarn over and around the tip of the right-hand needle.

3 Use the tip of the right-hand needle to draw the loop through the stitch. Slip the original stitch off the left-hand needle to complete the first purl stitch.

Repeat these three steps until all the stitches on the left-hand needle have been transferred to the right-hand needle. At the end of the row, swap the needles so that all the stitches are again in your left hand.

CONTINENTAL STYLE: PURL STITCH

This is how you make a purl stitch using this method.

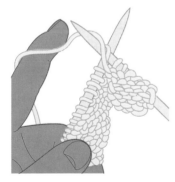 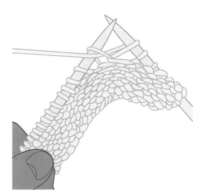 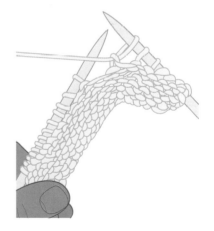

1 Hold the needle with the stitches to be purled in your left hand. Insert the tip of the right-hand needle into the front of the first stitch from right to left. Holding the yarn fairly taut at the back of your work, use the tip of the right-hand needle to pick up a loop of yarn.

2 With the tip of the right-hand needle, draw the yarn through the original stitch to form a loop

3 Slip the original stitch off the left-hand needle by gently pulling the right-hand right needle to the right. Repeat these three steps until all the stitches on the left-hand needle have been transferred to the right-hand needle. At the end of the row, swap the needles so that all the stitches are again in your left hand.

BINDING (CASTING) OFF

This is done to secure the final edge of the knitting so that it will not come undone. If you have been working a stitch pattern (see page 116), then work each stitch as it presents, so knit a knit stitch and purl a purl stitch as you bind (cast) off.

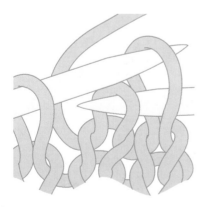

1 Work the first two stitches. *Insert the tip of the left-hand needle into the first stitch on the right-hand needle and lift this stitch over the second stitch and off the needle. Work the next stitch on the left-hand needle so that there are again two stitches on the right-hand needle*. Repeat from * until only one stitch remains.

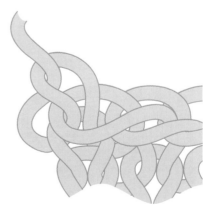

2 Cut the yarn leaving a 4in (10cm) tail and slip the final stitch off the needle. Draw the yarn tail through the stitch and pull the tail to tighten the stitch.

SHAPING

Through increasing and decreasing the number of stitches you can shape a piece of knitting. Different methods are used because they make the stitches slope in different directions to create a neater look.

Increasing This involves creating new stitches in a row to make the knitting wider. There are two methods of increasing that appear in the projects in this book.

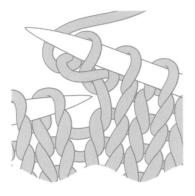

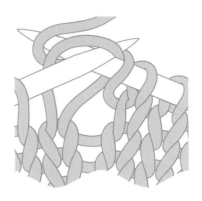

Increase (inc) Knit the stitch in the usual way, but without dropping the original stitch off the left-hand needle. Now knit into the back of the same stitch and drop the original off the left-hand needle as usual. You are creating a new stitch by knitting one stitch twice.

Yarnover (yo) Create an extra stitch by passing the yarn over the right-hand needle between stitches. When knitting, bring the yarn between the point of the two needles, then over the right-hand needle and to the back, ready to knit the next stitch, as shown here. When purling, wrap the yarn all the way around the needle so that it comes back in front where it needs to be to purl the next stitch. On the next row, treat this new stitch in the same way as all other stitches.

Decreasing This involves reducing the number of stitches in a row to make the knitting narrower. There are several methods of decreasing used in this book.

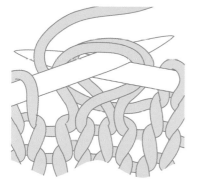

Knit two together (k2tog) Insert the right-hand needle knitwise through the front of the next two stitches on the left-hand needle and knit them together as though they were one stitch. Slip both stitches off the left-hand needle, leaving one stitch on the right-hand needle.

Knit two together through the back loops (k2togtbl) This is worked in a similar way to k2tog, but instead of inserting the right needle into the stitches from front to back, you insert it from right to left, through the back of the two stitches, and then you knit them together. It is a little fiddlier to accomplish but works well when teamed with k2tog to create symmetrical decreases.

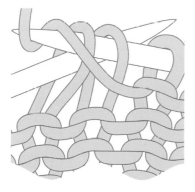

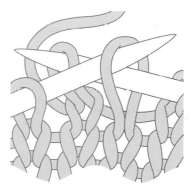

Purl two together (p2tog) Insert the right-hand needle purlwise through the front of the next two stitches on the left-hand needle and purl them together as though they were one stitch. Slip both stitches off the left-hand needle, leaving one stitch on the right-hand needle.

Similarly, if instructed to purl 3 together (p3tog), repeat as above but insert the right-hand needle through three stitches rather than two.

Slip one, knit one, pass the slipped stitch over (skpo) Insert the right-hand needle knitwise into the next stitch and slip it directly onto that needle, without actually knitting it. Knit the next stitch as usual. Using the tip of the left-hand needle, lift the slipped stitch over the knitted one and drop it off the right-hand needle.

SLIPPING, ELONGATING, AND DROPPING STITCHES

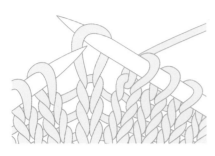

Slip one (Sl1) Insert the right needle (from back to front) into the next stitch on the left needle and place it on the right needle without working it.

Slip one stitch purlwise with yarn in front (sl1 wyf) Bring the yarn between the needles to the front of the knitting before slipping a stitch from the left needle to the right, and when slipping the stitch insert the right needle through the front of the stitch to be slipped, as though working a purl stitch. Finally, take the yarn between the needles to the back of the knitting.

Slip one stitch purlwise with yarn at back (sl1 wyb) This is worked in the same way as above but take the yarn between the needles to the back of the knitting before slipping the stitch, then return it to the front.

Wrapping yarn twice around needle / Elongated stitch (K1 wy2/P1 wy2)
Row 1: Insert right hand needle into the stitch and wrap the yarn around the needle twice. Pull the wrapped yarn through the stitch as you would with a normal knit or purl stitch.
Row 2: Work into each elongated stitch as you would normally, picking up only one wrap and letting the other drop off the needle.

Dropping a stitch Although this usually happens as a mistake, there are occasions when a pattern will call for you to drop a stitch off your left-hand needle on purpose (such as the Linen scarf on page 68). Simply slide the stitch to be dropped off your needle and continue knitting the remaining stitches as per the pattern instructions.

WORKING IN PATTERN

You will find the phrase "work every st in patt as it presents" in many patterns in this book, and it means that you need to work the stitches in the pattern set on previous rows.

The simplest way to understand this is that if the next stitch on the left-hand needle looks like a knit stitch (it is a V shape), then you should knit it. If it looks like a purl stitch (it is a little bump), then you should purl it. Once you've worked a couple of rows, the stitch pattern will be established and will be easy to see.

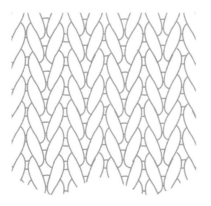

Stockinette (stocking) stitch is made by knitting and purling entire alternate rows.

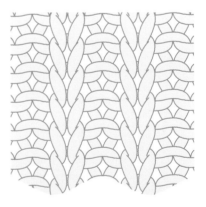

Rib is made by knitting and purling alternate stitches on every row; working each stitch as it presents will create columns of knit and purl stitches.

CABLES

Create texture and pattern by swapping the order in which you knit stitches. Cables are much simpler to work than you might at first think, and using a bent cable needle (see page 104) will make it even easier to hold the group of stitches being moved.

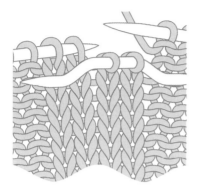

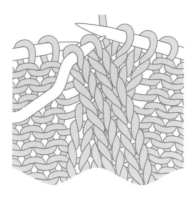

Cable four forward (C4F)

1 Work to the position of the cable. Slip the next two stitches on the left-hand needle onto the cable needle and hold it at the front of the work.

2 Knit the next two stitches off the left-hand needle in the usual way, then knit the two stitches off the cable needle.

Cable six forward (C6F)

As above, but hold three stitches at the front on the cable needle.

Cable twelve forward (C12F)

As above, but hold six stitches at the front on the cable needle.

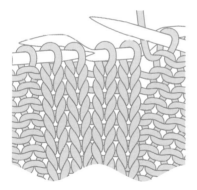

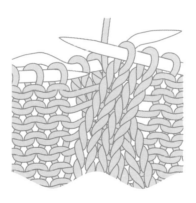

Cable four back (C4B)

1 Work to the position of the cable. Slip the next two stitches on the left-hand needle onto the cable needle and hold it at the back of the work.

2 Knit the next two stitches off the left-hand needle in the usual way, then knit the two stitches off the cable needle.

Cable twelve back (C12B) As above, but hold six stitches at the back on the cable needle.

Cable three left (C3L) Work to the position of the cable. Slip the next two stitches on the left-hand needle onto the cable needle and hold it at the front of the work. Purl the next stitch off the left-hand needle in the usual way, then knit the two stitches off the cable needle.

Cable three right (C3R) Work to the position of the cable. Slip the next stitch on the left-hand needle onto the cable needle and hold it at the back of the work. Knit the next two stitches off the left-hand needle in the usual way, then purl the single stitch off the cable needle.

KNITTING IN THE ROUND

This is a method of knitting using double-pointed needles (or a circular needle) to work continuously around the stitches to create a seamless tube.

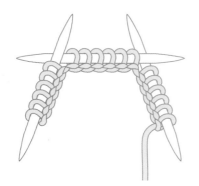

1 Cast on the required number of stitches onto one double-pointed needle. Slip some stitches from either end onto two more needles so that there are an equal number of stitches on three needles. Check that the stitches all lie flat and that this cast-on row is not twisted.

2 Use a stitch marker, or a loop of contrast yarn: this marker will just be passed from one needle to another to mark the start of each round. Using the fourth needle, knit the first cast-on stitch, pulling the yarn tightly so that the three original needles form a triangle. Knit all the stitches off the first needle. Using this newly free needle, knit all the stitches off the second needle, and then knit them all off the third. Once you have knitted all the stitches off all three needles in turn, you have completed one round of knitting.

PICKING UP STITCHES

In order to continue knitting but in a different direction, you need to pick up stitches along a side edge of a completed piece of knitting.

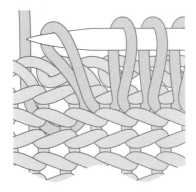

With the right side of the work facing you, insert a knitting needle into the knitted fabric between the edge stitch and the next stitch along on the first row. Wrap the yarn knitwise around the tip of the needle. Pull through a loop, so creating a new stitch on the knitting needle. Repeat the process along the edge to pick up the required number of stitches, making sure you space them evenly.

CHANGING COLORS

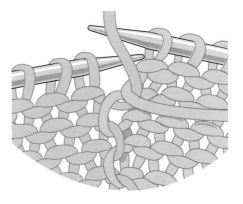

You can loop the yarns around one another if the colors change in a straight line up the work. If you are working stripes, change color at the end of row by dropping the old color at the end of the row and knitting the new color at the beginning of the row. You can either cut the old color, leaving a 6in (15cm) tail for sewing in later, or—if the color changes fall on an even number—you can weave the yarns up the side of the work by winding them round each other, looping them up the side as you knit.

TO MAKE UP

It's important to finish and sew up your projects as carefully as you knitted them for a good-looking result. Mattress stitch is worked on the right side of the knitting and allows you to perfectly match a stitch pattern or stripes.

Loose ends Weave in the tails of yarn from casting on and binding (casting) off to create a neat and secure finish. Using a tapestry needle, sew the tail up and down through the backs of at least five stitches across a row. Do not pull the tail tight or the knitting will pucker.

Sewing seams Generally it is best to use the same yarn to join seams that you have used for knitting, but if the knitting is particularly chunky try using a finer yarn in the same color. Use a tapestry needle when sewing seams—a blunt-ended tip is best because it is less likely to split the yarn. Use a piece of yarn no longer than 18–24in (45–60cm), because a longer piece may start to tangle and knot. Make sure you have plenty of light before sewing up.

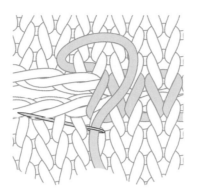

Mattress stitch on cast-on and bound-(cast-) off edges Lay the two pieces right-side up with the edges to be joined touching. Thread a tapestry needle with a length of the project yarn (or yarn in a matching color if the project yarn is not very strong). Secure the yarn on the back of the upper piece, at one end of the seam. Bring yarn through to the front between the first and second stitch of the first row. Insert the needle between the first and second stitch of the first row on the other piece. Pass the needle under both strands of the second stitch and back through to the front. Insert the needle into the same hole it emerged from on the first piece and pass it under both strands of the second stitch and back through to the front. Repeat this process, zig-zagging from one piece to the other and always taking the needle under both strands of the next stitch along. After every two or three stitches, pull up the yarn gently to close the seam.

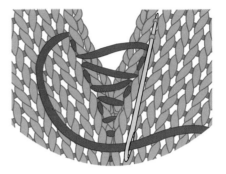

Mattress stitch on row ends Lay the two pieces right-side up with the edges to be joined touching. Secure the yarn on the back of the right-hand piece, at the bottom of the seam. Bring the yarn through to the front between the first and second stitch of the first row. Insert the needle between the first and second stitch of the first row on the other piece. Pass the needle upward, under the horizontal strand of yarn between the first and second stitch, then under the same strand in the row above, and bring it through back to the front. Insert the needle into the same hole it emerged from on the first piece and pass it upward under the corresponding horizontal strands. Repeat this process, zig-zagging from one side to the other and always taking the needle under two horizontal strands. After every two or three stitches, pull up the yarn gently to close the seam.

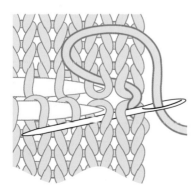

Grafting/Kitchener stitch This technique copies the shape of the knitted stitch, making a seamless join and works best when joining stockinette (stocking) stitch.

Put each line of stitches on a needle (without binding/casting off) or on stitch holders. Work as for mattress stitch, weaving the thread from one piece to the other and working stitch to stitch.

TROUBLESHOOTING

Holding a stitch Keep a safety pin or a stitch holder pinned to the top of your knitting project bag so that it's to hand in case of a dropped stitch emergency. Put the pin or holder through the stitch loop as soon as you can to stop it unraveling any further while you get ready to pick it up.

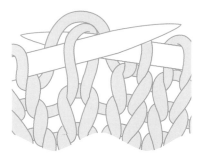

Picking up a stitch dropped in the row you are knitting Insert the right-hand needle into the loop of the dropped stitch and under the strand it has dropped from. Use the tip of the left-hand needle to pass the stitch over the strand, dropping the stitch and pulling the loop of the strand through. Ensure that the stitch is lying on the left-hand needle and is facing in the correct direction, then continue knitting.

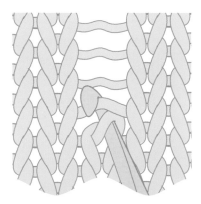

Picking up a dropped stitch from several rows below Insert a crochet hook into the loop of the dropped stitch at the bottom of the ladder that has appeared. Catch the strand lying directly above it and draw this strand through the loop. Continue in this way up the ladder until all the strands have been caught, then slip the final loop onto the left-hand needle.

GAUGE (TENSION)

To ensure that your finished knitting is the correct size, it is imperative to knit a gauge (tension) swatch that you can check against the details given in the pattern you have chosen. The gauge is given as the number of stitches in a 4 x 4in (10 x 10cm) square.

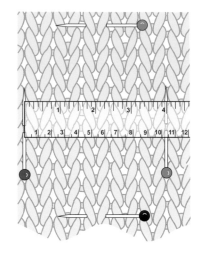

Using the recommended yarn and needles, cast on eight stitches more than the gauge (tension) instruction asks for (so if you need to have 10 stitches to 4in (10cm), cast on 18 stitches). Working in pattern as instructed, work eight rows more than is needed. Bind (cast) off loosely.

• Lay the swatch flat without stretching it (the gauge is given before washing or felting). Lay a ruler across the stitches with the 2in (5cm) mark centered on the knitting, then put a pin in the knitting at the start of the ruler and at the 4in (10cm) mark: the pins should be well away from the edges of the swatch. Count the number of stitches between the pins. Repeat the process across the rows to count the number of rows to 4in (10cm).

• If the number of stitches and rows you've counted is the same as the number asked for in the instructions, you have the correct gauge (tension). If you do not have the same number then you will need to change your gauge (tension). Don't just try to knit to a different gauge (tension): everyone has a "natural" gauge (tension) and if you try to knit tighter or looser it won't be consistent and you will simply end up with uneven knitting. To change gauge (tension) you need to change the size of your knitting needles. A good rule of thumb to follow is that one difference in needle size will create a difference of one stitch in the gauge (tension). You will need to use larger needles to achieve fewer stitches and smaller ones to achieve more stitches, so if you have one too many stitches, knit another swatch with needles one size larger. If you have one too few stitches, use needles one size smaller.

• Work swatches until you have the right gauge (tension): it might seem a bit time-consuming, but it's better then knitting a whole project and than finding out that it's the wrong size.

SUBSTITUTING YARN

If you want to change the yarn, then you need to work out how many balls to buy.

• Choose a substitute yarn that is the same thickness as the pattern yarn or you'll end up with a project that's an entirely different size. Balls of two different brands of the same type of yarn won't necessarily contain the same quantity of yarn, even if the balls weigh the same. It's the yardage (meterage) in a ball, not the weight that's important.

• Different yarns may not knit up to the same gauge (tension). The yarn wrapper on the substitute yarn should give you its standard gauge (tension), and as long as this isn't different from the pattern yarn gauge (tension) by more than a stitch or row, or two, you should be able to get the right gauge (tension) (see opposite).

• Before buying all the substitute yarn, buy just one ball and knit a gauge (tension) swatch to be absolutely certain that you can get the right gauge (tension) with that yarn.

• If the substitute yarn has a different yardage (meterage) per ball to the pattern yarn, then you need to do a sum to work out how many balls to buy.

• Multiply the yardage (meterage) in one ball of pattern yarn by the number of balls needed to find out the total yardage (meterage) of yarn required.

• Then divide the total yardage (meterage) by the yardage (meterage) in one ball of the substitute yarn to find out how many balls of that yarn you need to buy.

Example:
The pattern yarn has 109yds (100m) of yarn in each ball and you need 13 balls.
109 (100) x 13 = 1417yds (1300m) of yarn needed in total.

The substitute yarn has 123yds (112m) of yarn in each ball.
1417 ÷ 123 = 11.52
(1300 ÷ 112 = 11.6)
So you only need to buy 12 balls of the substitute yarn.

SUGGESTED YARN SUBSTITUTES FOR THE PROJECTS IN THIS BOOK

Super chunky yarn designed to be knitted on size US 15 (10mm) or US 17 (12mm) needles:
• Magnum from Cascade
• Crazy Sexy Wool from Wool and the Gang

Stretchy jersey fabric yarn:
• Tek Tek
• Hoopla from Hoopla
• Boodles from Hobbycraft
• Noodles yarn from Sullivans

Mega chunky yarn, designed to be knitted on size US 50 (25mm) needles or larger
• Fat Bubba by Melanie Porter
• Fat and Sassy Merino from Tjockt
• Big Stitch from Bagsmith
• Big Wool from Loopy Mango

MAKE YOUR OWN FAT YARN FROM WOOL ROVING

Preparing the roving properly is very important as it makes it strong enough for knitting. You do not want to felt the fibers, but the roving should feel like it has puffed up slightly, with a firmer handle.

1 Place a double sheet flat on the floor. Starting in one corner and pulling the roving out of the bag as you go, lay a continuous length of roving along one side, following the edge of the sheet. When you reach the opposite corner, don't break off the roving but fold the sheet over to fully cover the wool, then lay another line of roving parallel to the previous length. Continue in this way until you have fully laid out and wrapped as much roving as will fit on the sheet, ensuring that the sheet fabric is always separating the lengths of roving so that they will not felt together. Tie a length of string every 8in (20cm) down the bundle to hold it closed. Start a new sheet and wrap more roving in the same way until you have prepared all the roving in the bags.

2 Fill the bathtub with the hottest tap water possible and put in as much washing detergent as for a normal single load in your washing machine. Lay the bundles in the hot water. Wearing rubber boots, climb into the bathtub and stomp on the bundles for about five minutes to encourage a certain amount of felting. Drain the water, then rinse the bundles several times to remove any trace of detergent.

3 Spin the bundles if you have a washing machine, or squeeze them until you have removed as much water as possible if you do not. Open the bundles and lay the now slightly felted wool on a drying rack for at least 12 hours to dry. Repeat until you have prepared all the roving.

4 Once the wool is fully dry, pull the end of one length apart so that the roving is split evenly in two: as you gently pull, the roving should easily split down the entire length. Roll the newly created yarn into balls ready to knit.

MAKING HANDMADE FABRIC YARN

There are two different methods of fabric cutting used in this book. The bias cut is used for the linen shrug (page 74) and linen scarf (page 68). The straight cut is for the cotton bracelets (page 44) and cotton top (page 71).

Straight cut

Cut around the piece of fabric, from the outside in, in a spiral to make continuous strip.

Bias cut

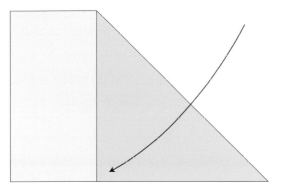

1 Lay a rectangle of fabric out flat, then fold the top edge over to create a diagonal fold.

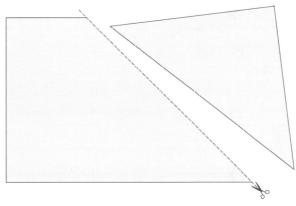

2 Cut along the diagonal fold, and place the triangular piece to one side.

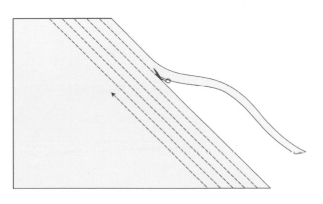

3 Cut parallel strips of the required width diagonally across the fabric.

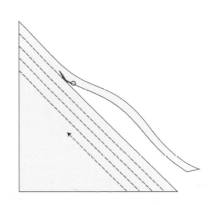

4 Repeat on the triangular piece.

ABBREVIATIONS

approx	approximately
alt	alternate; alternatively
beg	begin(s)(ning)
C4B	cable four stitches (or number stated) back
C4F	cable four stitches (or number stated) front
cont	continue
g	gram(s)
inc	increase
k	knit
k2tog	knit two stitches (or number stated) together
k2togtbl	knit 2 sts together through the back loops
LH	left-hand
m	meters
mm	millimeters
oz	ounce(es)
p	purl
p2tog	purl two stitches (or number stated) together
rem	remain(ing)
rep	repeat
rev st st	reverse stockinette (stocking) stitch
RH	right-hand
RS	right side
skpo	slip 1, knit 1, pass slipped stitch over
sl1	slip 1 stitch
sl1 wyb	slip 1 st with yarn at back
sl1 wyf	slip 1 st with yarn at front
st(s)	stitch(es)
st st	stockinette (stocking) stitch
tog	together
WS	wrong side
wyb	with yarn at back
wyf	with yarn in front
yo	yarn over
[ ]	repeat instructions inside [ ] as given
* *	repeat instructions between * * as given

KNITTING NEEDLE SIZES

There are three systems of sizing knitting needles, and not every size exists in every system. This chart compares sizes across the three systems.

US	Metric	old UK and Canadian
120	35mm	—
50	25mm	—
35	19mm	—
19	15mm	—
17	12mm	—
15	10mm	000
13	9mm	00
11	8mm	0
11	7.5mm	1
10½	7mm	2
10½	6.5mm	3
10	6mm	4
9	5.5mm	5
8	5mm	6
7	4.5mm	7
6	4mm	8
5	3.75mm	9
4	3.5mm	—
3	3.25mm	10
2/3	3mm	11
2	2.75mm	12
1	2.25mm	13
0	2mm	14
00	1.75mm	—
000	1.5mm	—

Resources

YARNS

Cascade Yarns
US: www.cascadeyarns.com
UK: www.loveknitting.com

Hobby Craft
www.hobbycraft.co.uk

Hoopla
US: www.jonesandvandermeer.com
UK: www.creative-you.co.uk

Lion Brand Yarns
US: www.lionbrand.com
UK: www.loveknitting.com

Loopy Mango
US: www.loopymango.com
UK: www.loveknitting.com

Melanie Porter
www.melanieporter.com

Rowan Yarns
Green Lane Mill
Holmfirth
West Yorkshire
England
HD9 2DX
www.knitrowan.com

The Bagsmith
24000 Mercantile Road
Suite 7
Beachwood
OH 44122
United States
www.bagsmith.com

SPECIFIC PROJECT MATERIALS

Bespoke giant knitting needles
www.melanieporter.com
www.tjockt.com
www.gogirlknitting.com

Bag handles
www.joann.com
www.hobbycraft.co.uk

Index

Acknowledgments

I would like to thank the following people for their help and contributions:

My husband Vik and son Jai, neither of whom remotely understand what I'm talking about, but smile and encourage me nonetheless.

With many thanks to Cindy Richards and the team at CICO Books for commissioning this book and in particular to Carmel Edmonds for her constant reassurances and help. Thank you to Katy Denny and to Susan Horan for tirelessly checking my ramblings and patterns, and to stylist Nel Haynes and photographers Penny Wincer and Emma Mitchell for creating gorgeous photographs.

Cascade Yarns, Hoopla, Bagsmith, and Lion Brand kindly supplied fantastic yarns for me to work with for the book.

And finally I would like to thank my mum, without whom I would never have been able to complete this book.